The Music Business Advice Book

*150 Immediately Useful
Tips From The Pros*

Bobby Owsinski

The Music Business Advice Book

150 Immediately Useful Tips From The Pros
by Bobby Owsinski

Published by:
Bobby Owsinski Media Group
4109 West Burbank, Blvd.
Burbank, CA 91505

© Bobby Owsinski 2018
ISBN 13: 978-1-946837-00-4

Please note that much of this publication is based on personal experience and anecdotal evidence. Although the author and publisher have made every reasonable attempt to achieve complete accuracy of the content in this Book, they assume no responsibility for errors or omissions.

Also, you should use this information as you see fit, and at your own risk. Your particular situation may not be exactly suited to the examples illustrated herein; in fact, it's likely that they won't be the same, and you should adjust your use of the information and recommendations accordingly.

Any trademarks, service marks, product names or named features are assumed to be the property of their respective owners, and are used only for reference. There is no implied endorsement if we use one of these terms.

Finally, nothing in this Book is intended to replace common sense, legal, medical or other professional advice, and is meant to inform and entertain the reader.

To buy books in quantity for corporate use or incentives, call 818.588.6606 or email office@bobbyowsinski.com.

Table Of Contents

3. Play Well With Others 67

4. Educate Yourself 119

Introduction

Everyone who's ever made a living in the music business has learned a number of lessons along the way, and it's almost guaranteed that at least some of them have been hard. The good thing is that if we having any staying power in the business, we learn from those mistakes and come out the other side even stronger than before.

A few of us are fortunate in that there's been a strong mentor in our life that passes on the benefit of his or her long career to us. To many that's a shortcut that saves years of painful searching for answers, but the problem is that kind of opportunity is only available to a lucky and select few.

Regardless of how we learned these lessons, they're nonetheless valuable to not only those starting out in the business, but those who have already put their years in. After all, it doesn't matter when we receive the advice that might turn on the lightbulb, it's the fact that it comes at all (I can testify to that personally, since a number of things in this book proved to be a lightbulb moment for me too).

I've always been fascinated by talking to people in the music industry, and over the course of 20 years or so I've managed to do maybe a thousand or so interviews with musicians, artists, engineers, producers, songwriters, publishers, label execs and others working in the music business for magazine articles, books, and most recently my *Inner Circle Podcast*. The interesting thing is that there's usually a similarity in their stories about how they came to work in the industry, yet there's a uniqueness to each one, frequently from way out of left field.

Very early on at the end of each Podcast episode I began to ask my guest the same final question: *What is the best piece of business advice that you learned along the way in your career, or that someone imparted to you?* This book is a compilation of those answers.

You'll see a few common themes in most of the answers, but there will be some surprises as well. Either way, you'll find the advice we'll worth the read, and an excellent blueprint for either a new career, or to take a current one to the next level.

The contributors in this book come from the following areas of the music business:

- Music Production
- Music Business
- Post-Production
- Technology
- Music Publishing
- Artist Management

As you read, you'll notice that there are also a number of recurring themes. These include:

- Follow your passion
- Play well with others
- The value of networking
- Taking care of business
- Educate yourself
- Own your content
- Getting paid
- and finally, music gems of wisdom

Truly there's a piece of advice for everyone in this book and I must admit that after all these years in the business, I was just as affected by a few that struck home to me as I think you will be as well.

Indeed your life may be changed by a well-placed jewel of information as you read the words of wisdom from these industry veterans.

The Contributors

Many thanks to everyone who contributed to this book. Some fall into several categories, but they're listed here in the context of their advice.

Engineers

Owen Curtin
Lij Shaw
Chris SD
Bob Brockman
Bob Bullock
Ross Hogarth
Richard Chycki
Elliot Scheiner
John Jaszcz
Bubba Sellito
Josh Gudwin
Joe Chiccarelli
Tim Latham
Mark Frink
JJ Blair
Tony Shepperd
Tom Weir
Gary Noble
Drew Drucker
Wyn Davis
Barry Rudolph

Andrew Scheps
Vance Powell
Francis Buckley
Phil Rohr
Larry Crane
Jordan Young
Josh Williams
Eric "Mixerman" Sarafin
Michael Bishop
Billy Decker
Ed Seay
Dave Pensado
Garth Richardson
Sylvia Massy
Bob Power
Joel Hamilton
Bill Smith
Dennis Moody
Ed Cherney
Dave Hampton
Jeri Palumbo

Mastering Engineers

Pete Doell
Gavin Lurssen
Ian Shepherd

Pete Lyman
John Greenham

Producers

Ken Calliat
Ted Hutt
Michael Beinhorn
John Kurzwig
Mike Elizondo

Bob Margouleff
Eric Copeland
Rob Schnapf
Warren Huart

Post-Production

Scott Gershin

Jason Brennan

Nick Peck

Brian Schmidt

Mike Rodriguez

Michael Perricone

Alex Benyon

Musicians

Pete Thorn

Mark Shulman

Stevie Black

Stonebridge

Dennis Dreith

Joe Sublett

Scott Page

Chris "Manifest" Greenwood

Shane Theriot

Dusty Wakeman

Jamie Oldaker

Kellii Scott

Gary Solt

Paul ILL

Composers/Songwriters

Rich Walters

David Campos

Chris Boardman

Diego Stucco

Rich Tozzoli

Clarence Jey

Michael Carey

Carmen Rizzo

Richard Gibbs

Martin Page

Bobby Summerfield

Rob Artbitier

Management

Candace Stewart

Nicholas Mishko

Mike Gormley

Antony Bland

John Mathiason

Steve Marcone

David Philip

Rick Barker

Walter Turbitt

Jay Coyle

Chandler Coyle

Music Publishing

Jamie Purpora   Greig Watts

Joyce Kettering

Record Label

Shawn Mikle

Shan Dan Horan

Technology

Steven Slate   Dirk Ulrich

Michael Carnes   Gary Myerberg

Gebre Wadell   Chris Crawford

David Bock   Ben Loftus

Bob Hodas   Roy LaManna

Jeff Ponchick   Russ Hughes

John Jennings   Matt Hines

Hanson Hsu   Joey Sturgis

Roger Linn   Dane Meyers

Music Business

Dae Bogen   John Kellogg

Ariel Hyatt   Daryl Friedman

Tommy Darker   Ellis Sorkin

Dave Kusek   Denny Tedesco

Frank Wells   David Alexander

Bryan Calhoun   David Scheirman

1

Follow Your Passion

You've probably heard that if you follow your passion that everything in your life will work out fine. You might also believe that this advice doesn't even seem possibe from where you now sit.

Following your passion to success doesn't usually happen overnight unfortunately, but the observations that you read next may give you another way to look at what it takes to pursue your career.

Eat It, Live It, Breath It

#1: Scott Gershin

Scott Gershin is an award-winning sound designer who has taken audiences on immersive journeys for three decades on films such as *Nightcrawler, Pacific Rim, Hellboy 2, Star Trek* and *American Beauty* and games like *Doom, Epic Mickey, Gears of War, Resident Evil* and *Fable*. Scott has been recognized multiple times by MPSE, GANG, NAMM Foundation, BAFTA, DICE, and the Academy of Motion Picture Arts and Sciences. His advice comes from Inner Circle Podcast #44.

Scott: I think it comes down to this - what's the secret to success? Quite a bit of insanity actually. I think you've got to be a little crazy. Ultimately all of us that went into the entertainment business had our families plead with us not to do it.

I've had relatives say to me, "You're in the business. Tell so and so he shouldn't do it." [laughs] But it all comes down to if you have a passion, regardless of what you're doing in the creative arts. It's going to be hard, but you don't care. It's what you want to do. It's what you have to do.

> *...people really love people who care*
> *and have a love for what they're doing,*
> *or what you're doing.*

I keep thinking, "Oh my God. What am I going to do when I have to get an actual job?", because even today I still feel like I'm playing. I feel fortunate with what I do. I feel passion. We're going to put hours in and the pressure's going to be so high, and everything is on the line because everything you do is judged by the last thing you've done.

Love what you do. Be passionate about what you do. Submerse yourself in it. It should be everything to you, especially when you're young and before you get into any kind of a relationship. It is what you do, and hopefully the person who is with you goes for the ride.

Prepare for the insecurities. It goes from, "Oh, my God. This is great." to "I'm never going to work again." You go through these little creative swings, but ultimately it comes down to that you've got to care, and people really love people who care and have a love for what they're doing, or what you're doing. If there's a single thing I could tell people, it would be to eat it, live it, and breath it.

———

Do What You Believe In

#2: David Alexander

Icon Collective is one of the coolest music production schools anywhere, teaching students not only how to make their way in the world of electronic music but how to also think like entrepreneurs. Co-founder David Alexander has a background as a touring musician, a producer, and composer on hit video games like *Quake II* and *III* and *James Bond 007*. His advice comes from Inner Circle Podcast #56.

David: One that resonates with me right now is how much faith you need to have in what you're trying to accomplish. It's the idea that you have to believe in what your doing first before anyone else believes it.

A lot of times we pursue an idea and we look for other people to validate it before we move forward, but life works just the opposite. You have to be the one to validate and believe in what you're doing, and then people will get behind you as if you're already at your goal. I think that's one of the biggest lessons.

> *You have to be the one to validate and believe in what you're doing, and then people will get behind you as if you're already at your goal.*

I actually learned that at a seminar that I was recording before we started the school. I had to listen to the presentation to make sure that there were no glitches in the audio. One guy said, "You don't have to be at your destination. You just have to be walking towards its so strongly that people will get behind you as if you're already there." And I never forgot that.

I have to believe in what I want to do before other people believe it. I think that applies to anything you're trying to do, whether you're creative or in business or in any other type of strategy.

From that lesson I surmised that Icon Collective would be a reality if I spoke confidently about its inception. Instead of saying, "We're thinking of starting a school in April," we started saying, "In April Icon Collective *will* launch."

This simple change in perspective and vocabulary had a tremendous impact on the people we spoke with. They believed, without a doubt, that Icon Collective would be a reality as well, and that allowed each person to equally commit to the idea.

As a matter of fact, when we began speaking of Icon Collective in the affirmative, we didn't have a location or even students. It was the declaration of belief that it would happen which allowed us to obtain both the location and the students. People got behind the idea even though we were not at our goal yet.

Belief followed by speaking your belief in the affirmative, become very powerful tools in manifesting your vision.

———

Don't Give Up

#3: Denny Tedesco

The Wrecking Crew was one of the greatest group of studio musicians ever assembled. During the 1960s and 70s they played on just about every hit record, television show and movie that came out of Los Angeles, including hits by Phil Spector, The Beach Boys, Mamas and Papas, Cher, Simon and Garfunkel and many more. Denny Tedesco is the director of the film *The Wrecking Crew* that documents the group's rise and fall. His father was the famed studio guitarist Tommy Tedesco, a main member of the Crew. His advice comes from Inner Circle Podcast #61 and focuses on the difficulty he had getting music clearances for the film.

Denny: If you really believe in something, don't give up. When the doors were closed, I'd go through a window. When the window was closed, I'd go through a door.

My dad taught me one thing. He said, "Never blow up on a leader," meaning that you could be 110 percent right, but if you blow up on the boss, don't expect to come back to work tomorrow.

> *...you could be 110 percent right, but if you blow up on the boss, don't expect to come back to work tomorrow*

There were times over the 19 years making this film that I wanted to scream at a label guy or a publisher, and I didn't. I just sucked it up, because I knew that sooner or later they'd be on my side. In many cases, they don't forget the hell they've put you through.

———

The Difference Is The Hours

#4: Gary Solt

Gary Solt has been the favorite guitar player for orchestra recording sessions for dozens of movies and television shows, and has toured North America and Japan as a featured guitarist with the Percy Faith Orchestra, Don Rader, Leslie Uggams, Shirley Bassey, the Bruce Paulson L.A. All-Star Big Band, among many others. His advice comes from Inner Circle Podcast #72.

Gary: I had a guitar teacher a long time ago who could play stuff that I had no idea how he was doing it. I kept on asking, "How do you do that? Show me that lick? How do I play that?" I would say, "How come I can't do that?" His answer to me was as right as the day is long. He said, "You know, the only difference between you and me is hours. If you put in the time, you'll always be able to move forward and you'll always be able to do what you want to do."

So my advice is to put in as many hours as you possibly can. That's what separates you from the seasoned guys out there who are doing it, because all they've done for years and years is do what they do for hours and hours and hours. If you do that, you've got a shot.

If you put in the time, you'll always be able to move forward and you'll always be able to do what you want to do.

Don't Compromise

#5: Pete Thorn

Pete Thorn has played with superstars like Don Henley, Chris Cornell, Melissa Ethridge, Robbie Draco Rosa and Jewel, and has recorded with James Blunt, Daniel Powter, Alicia Keys, Pink, among many others. He also writes a monthly column in Premier Guitar magazine called *Tone Tips From The Road*, and has a highly regarded YouTube channel filled with lesson videos and gear demonstrations. His advice comes from Inner Circle Podcast #76 and centers around his making that big move from his home in Canada to Los Angeles.

Pete: At some point I began to waver in my commitment to move to Los Angeles to attend Musicians Institute. My parents were great parents but they thought I'd be better off going to a more traditional college, and at some point my dad's fears began to get through to me.

I went to see Terry McDade, my guitar teacher at the time. He was one of the few musicians who was actually making a living at playing music in Edmonton, but he seemed to have the least amount of stress of anyone that I knew, and I took note of that. He looked at me and said, "You're really good at this, and you should really consider that before you make this decision."

He really believed in me and urged me to think about it a little bit more before I made up my mind. That's all I really needed to hear at that moment.

"I can tell you have a dream and what's in your heart so you should follow that. Don't compromise."

There are people that come along in your life and they can have a really big impact on you. A lot of decisions are made in an instant and that can change the course of your life, but it took for him to say, "You've got something special and you shouldn't give up on that."

Coming from a guy who was obviously happy and making a living in a city like Edmonton, which isn't a music center or anything, made me take that advice to heart and that was it. I was off after that.

He was saying, "I can tell you have a dream and what's in your heart so you should follow that. Don't compromise."

———

Stay The Course

#6: Robert Margouleff

Robert Margouleff has been super influential in that he was largely responsible for the synthesizer coming to the forefront of popular music, which led to co-producing four of Stevie Wonder's most beloved albums (including my personal favorites *Inner Visions* and *Talking Book*). Bob was also an early proponent of surround sound music, a torch he carries to this day with Headphone Surround. His advice comes from Inner Circle Podcast #78.

Robert: Stay the course and believe in yourself and what you have to offer the world. The new folk instrument to me is the laptop. People write on it and make music on it, but now the real trick is to get the music to the people who live it.

Back in the 70s, if you had local radio airplay the labels had a reasonable expectation that you would have some music that they could sell. We still have to have a similar expectation, but the gatekeepers are gone and you have to get out and do it for yourself first.

> *Stay the course and believe in yourself*
> *and what you have to offer the world.*

No one's going to jump on your bandwagon unless they're reassured that they'll be able to take something away from it in terms of a financial reward.

If you make good music and have something that touches people's hearts and minds, you will have success. You have the means to be your own record company.

That is the saving grace of the business today. You now can control the entire chain yourself and don't have to put your future in the hands of anyone else.

———

Be In Love With What You Do

#7: Kellii Scott

Kellii Scott has played with the band Failure on and off for over 20 years. He was also part of producer Lynda Perry's studio band, performing on records with Christina Aguilera, Pink, Hole, Faith Hill and many more. His advice comes from Inner Circle Podcast #82.

Kellii: As a player in the music business I would say that you should make certain that you love the business before you even consider moving forward. That's the thing that kept me going. For most of my career I barely made a dime. It was very early on that I asked myself, "I'm not going to be able to have an apartment, or a girlfriend, or all the things that normal people get to have. Do I love playing music enough for that to be okay?"

> *...you should make certain that you love the business before you even consider moving forward*

That for me was probably the most important knowledge that I imparted onto myself. I wouldn't change anything about my musical career. I don't think I've ever deserved anything more than just that. Being in love with what I do was enough to keep me doing it all these years.

――

Once You Dive In, Just Stay At It

#8: Robert "Bubba" Selitto

Saturday Night Live has been a television institution for a long time now, and it's always featured some of the highest profile, most cutting edge musical guests. My good buddy and Emmy-winner Robert "Bubba" Selitto has been mixing the house sound at SNL for more than 30 years now, and he has some great thoughts about what it takes to make it in the music business. His advice comes from Inner Circle Podcast #87.

Bubba: Persistence is more important than talent. It helps if you're talented, but you can acquire the talent later.

When I was at Berklee [College of Music], Tony Texiera (one of the teachers who taught the commercial writing class) said, "Never sell ties because if you start, that's what you'll end up doing the rest of your life."

So my advice is, once you dive in, just stay at it. If you want to be in the music business in any capacity, then don't do something else because then you drift off.

Persistence is more important than talent.

When I got out of Berklee I did what everybody else did and found myself a gig. I wanted to be a recording engineer but I found myself in live sound and said, "Okay, that's what I'll do."

I did a good job at it (I did a good job at recording too). I would go to studios around town and guys would go, "Do you think this is fun? Isn't it more fun to be in the middle of a live audience?", so everyone has a different perception of what is fun. I still think that 15 hours in the studio is a lot of fun [laughs].

I've had a great career. I cannot be disappointed in the way it went at all, but to me it's all thanks to being persistent.

You Have To Keep On Going

#9: Mike Gromely

Mike Gromely was head of PR for Mercury and A&M Records before he headed into management, where he worked with acts like The Bangles, Oingo Boingo, Wall of Voodoo and Danny Elfman. He now heads up the music consulting company LA Personal Development. His advice comes from Inner Circle Podcast #94.

Mike: One aspect of success is "Don't give up." A lot of people say that, but it's really, really difficult to not to want to give up sometimes. It can be just heartbreaking to an artist because of the all the rejection that can happen.

I hesitate to use the word "failure," because it's just not a failure if someone rejects something like a line they've written. The guts it takes to reveal that. Just do it sometime. Write some lyrics and send them to a musician and say, "Can you do something with this?"

I've done that more for the fun of it, but when I was actually sending the lyrics to somebody, I knew they could write back and say, "You're an idiot." [laughs]

You're revealing your soul, whether it's good or bad, and rejection is almost automatic except on rare occasions.

If you truly believe in what you can do, something's going to happen.

So you just have to keep on going and not give up. If you truly believe in what you can do, something's going to happen.

—

Think With The Long View

#10: John Kellogg

Music attorney John Kellogg has represented acts like Levert and The O'Jays before becoming assistant chair of the Music Business and Management department at Berklee College of Music. John knows the music business from an artist's perspective as well, since prior to becoming an attorney, he was a singer in the funk band Cameo. He's also the author of *Take Care of Your Music Business, 2nd Edition -Taking the Legal and Business Aspects You Need to Know to 3.0*. His advice comes from Inner Circle Podcast #104.

John: I think that you have to keep the proper perspective. You have to understand that you don't get into a position to where you can make a living from this business overnight. It's something that takes time to develop and you have to have the proper perspective in thinking that you're going to invest a lot of time and energy, it's going to seem like it may not be paying off.

You have to understand that you don't get into a position to where you can make a living from this business overnight.

I tell students, "The music industry has always been tough, but you have to hang in there. And if you hang in there and have powerful product, great songs and great live performances, you're going to be all right in this industry."

That was the best advice I got. Just think with the long view. I've been fortunate enough to have represented clients like the O'Jays, who've been in the industry 55 years. The guys are in their 70s and they're still out performing. You can have a long career if you look at everything with the proper perspective.

———

It Takes Patience

#11: Joey Sturgis

Producer/engineer and plugin developer Joey Sturgis created Joey Sturgis Tones, a company that makes some of my favorite DAW plugins. JST currently makes a wide variety of very interesting plugins guided by Joey's steady hand. His advice comes from Inner Circle Podcast #109.

Joey: This might be obvious, but maybe not. I think that success always looks really easy, but it never is.

From an outsider's perspective you see someone climbing the ladder and you think, "They must've had it really easy," or "They must be really talented," but in reality even if you do have it easy or are really talented, it's still chaos.

I think that success always looks really easy, but it never is.

It still takes a lot of patience and perseverance, like you just can't give up and you have to keep trying.

The Joy Of What You Do

#12: Ian Shepherd

Ian Shepherd is a British mastering engineer, plugin developer, and host of *The Mastering Show* podcast. He runs the Production Advice website and is the founder of Dynamic Range Day, an annual event raising awareness about the Loudness War. His advice comes from Inner Circle Podcast #112.

Ian: The big one for me is that you need to be passionate about what you do. I lost a major Blu-ray [authoring] client, and that was a really tough time for me because I didn't have my own mastering studio at that point. I got quite depressed about it and got into an argument online with a guy named Tony, who basically just caught me on a bad day.

He asked me what I was doing and I told him I was doing Blu-ray authoring. He said, "What? No mastering?" and I shot back, "No, I have to pay the bills. You don't understand what it's like."

I've found that whenever I go for the thing that really gets me excited, that I'm really interested in, that's when the success comes.

He apologized and then said, "I'm sorry, but it just seems like a waste of your skills." I kind of shouted back at him again, but in hindsight I realized that it was more about me and how I was feeling than what he was saying. He said, "Stop worrying about it. You could do a better job mastering on headphones than most people could in the best studio in the world."

I just sort of shrugged and got on with things from there, but about a week later, the guy who owns the studio I was using at the time sent me a mix over and said, "What do you think of this?". I said, "I think the mix sounds great, but in terms of mastering maybe you should try this, this and this - but ignore me because I'm just listening on headphones." He sent me this email back that said, "Damn you, you're right. I hate you. You always do that to me."

Those two things sort of locked together in my head and got me thinking that maybe I didn't need to have a full-blown super-expensive studio in order for me to use the skills and instincts that I had built up over the years.

It wasn't an overnight thing, but from there on I started focusing back on the mastering and doing less and less of the Blu-ray and DVD stuff, and as soon as I did that, everything started to click. That's when I wrote my first ebook, and that's when I began writing about the sort of stuff that I really cared about on my website.

Prior to that I had been very busy and been making a living, but I'd been really stressed, and actually pretty unhappy. In hindsight I think it was because I wasn't doing the thing that I was most passionate about.

It sounds a bit "new age" and stuff, but you do need to be careful. Lots of people say to "Do what you love," and there is a risk that if you do the thing that you love you might accidentally kill your enthusiasm for it, but that's not my experience. I've found that whenever I go for the thing that really gets me excited and I'm really interested in, that's when the success comes.

Those are the blog posts that people respond to, the videos that people love, and those are the albums that are a huge success. It's the ones where it's all about the enthusiasm and the joy of what you do.

———

Do This Because You Have To

#13: Steven Slate

Steven Slate's personal journey in the music business has gone from musician to engineer to manufacturing some of the coolest and most forward-thinking audio gear available today. He's currently the founder and CEO of the Slate Companies, which include Slate Drums, Slate Digital, Slate Media Technologies, and Audio Legends. His advice comes from Inner Circle Podcast #117.

Steven: I think the best piece of advice that I can give is that you've got to do music because you love it, not because you think it's going to make you a millionaire or make you famous. You've got to do music because you're so passionate about it that you can't do anything else.

> *You've got to do music because you're so passionate about it that you can't do anything else.*

There's nothing wrong with money, and there's nothing wrong with making a career out of it, but what comes first is a true passion and love and respect for the art. Once you have that, then you're willing to fight for it, and that's when you become successful. You have to do this because you have to.

———

Anything You Want To Do Is Possible

#14: Josh Gudwin

There are stars, then there are superstars, then there's Justin Bieber, who seems to shine brighter than all the rest. Justin's studio partner Josh Gudwin has been recording, mixing and even producing one of the biggest names in the entertainment universe. His advice comes from Inner Circle Podcast #138.

Josh: Without sounding cliche, anything you want to do is possible. In our industry you're on the fastest roller coaster, then you're going through a slow lazy river. When the roller coaster's going you have to go with it, but when you're in the lazy river, that's the time to regroup, relearn your skills, refine things and catch up with the life that you just missed because you worked six months straight.

It's hard to create a dynamic between your work life and your home life, which is a challenge because I love what I do so much that I'd spend my entire life just working on music given the opportunity. But at the same time there's more to life than just that.

> *In our industry you're either on the fastest roller coaster, then you're going through a slow lazy river.*

There are "ah ha" moments in your entire career. I'll probably be lying on my death bed and go, "Oh, so that's what that was (laughs)." I'll be trying to better myself and learn my craft until I'm dead.

The other thing is that I've been talking to a lot of masters in different fields because I think there's something to be learned from every single different profession. If I'm in need of inspiration I'll talk to one of my friends who are crushing it in some other completely different field.

———

Spend Your Time Wisely

#15: Mike Elizondo

Mike Elizondo is a musician, songwriter and producer who's worked with hit artists as diverse as Dr. Dre, Eminem, and 50 Cent, to Kieth Urban, Maroon 5 and Carrie Underwood, to Avenged Sevenfold and Mastadon. He was nominated for Producer of the Year in 2008, and has a ton of huge singles and albums to his credit. His advice comes from Inner Circle Podcast #140.

Mike: The biggest thing for me sounds like a cliche, but choose what you do with your time wisely. There's been periods of my life where I felt that I was searching for things and doing a lot of things that I didn't truly love, but I was doing it because it was a gig.

I realized that the sooner that you can get to the point where you're doing things that you really love or you're being honest with yourself about what it is you're supposed to be doing, that's when you start to have your most success in terms of feeling gratified creatively as well as monetarily.

You want to be in a creative situation where you're truly inspired by the people that you're working with and you're not just doing something because it's a gig, or you're chasing a hit even though musically it doesn't have anything to do with what you enjoy. I've learned to try to eliminate that.

... the sooner that you can get to the point where you're doing things that you really love or you're being honest with yourself that this is what you're supposed to be doing, I think that's when you start to have your most success.

I try to be honest with myself about doing the things that I think are great, and not waste my time with things that aren't going to help me be great. That's a lesson that I've learned from pretty much every exceptional artist that I've gotten to work with in various genres.

———

Pursue Your Passion

#16: Owen Curtin

Engineer and educator Owen Curtin has been on top of DIY audio gear trend, creating the successful *Audio Builders Workshop* that happens every 3 months or so in Boston, as well as running a successful studio business. His advice comes from Inner Circle Podcast #158.

Owen: The best thing for me has been to pursue my passions. When I get off-track from that life gets a little dull but when I'm interested in something and pursue that, good things have happened.

Recording and electronics started out as personal interests that evolved into the work I enjoy. I mean, I own a recording studio, not in L.A. or New York or Nashville, but in Boston. It's a really great music town, but it is not the place you go to get rich in the music world.

> *When I get off-track life gets a little dull, and when I'm interested in something and pursue that, good things have happened.*

In this industry, if you're not driven by passion, then what are you doing here? If you are driven by passion, that is the joy you take from the work.

———

Build Your Own Thing

#17: Eric Copeland

Eric Copeland has become one of the top Christian and jazz producers in the country, producing around 25 artists every year. His specialty is not just music, but guiding and growing artists thanks to his decades of experience in the music business. Eric also has a deep interest in music history and writes a blog called *Music History Matters*. His advice comes from Inner Circle Podcast #192.

Eric: There is one piece of advice that I wish I could go back and give myself at 18 or 19, and that is to just build your own thing. Don't wait for someone to recognize your genius - build the thing that you want to do and start doing it.

That's the thing that everyone is afraid to do. That doesn't mean that you have to quit your job and eat ramen, which I have done before by the way.

Don't wait for someone to recognize your genius - build the thing that you want to do and start doing it.

If someone could have told me that they could look at all my talents and said, "You can do this. You just have to find the people that need you to do it." That's true whether you're an artist, a songwriter, a producer, or an engineer.

Don't be afraid to build the thing that you want to build and take it out there. It's hard work, there's no doubt, but it's absolutely the thing that I wish someone would have told me.

Don't wait for someone to recognize your genius - build the thing that you want to do and start doing it.

———

Help Everybody Around You

#18: Lij Shaw

Lij Shaw is the host of a great podcast called *Recording Studio Rockstars,* and is the owner of the Toy Box Studio in Nashville, where he's been making records for the last 25 years. His advice comes from Inner Circle Podcast #202.

Lij: One of the best things that I learned was to just believe in myself. I've come to the realization that everything I've ever done that's gone well is something where I've acknowledged who I am and let myself come through and be as honestly me as possible.

I think in the beginning it was easy to be enthusiastic about what I loved but quickly keep that close to the chest and assume that what everyone else was doing was probably a little more important and I should probably just do that. Believing in yourself is a core thing that you really have to do.

Believing in yourself is a core thing that you really have to do.

A real core business lesson is that I'm going to make it my goal to help everybody around me as much as I can and help them achieve their goals while at the same time staying open to receiving.

in other words, instead of feeling that you have to go out and get the money, just go out and give, but make sure that you're open to receiving opportunity and income and reciprocation for all the giving that you do.

———

Say Yes And Figure It Out Afterwards

#19: Warren Huart

Warren Huart is a producer, musician, engineer and composer who's credits include The Fray, Aerosmith, Daniel Powter and Korn, among many others. His *Produce Like A Pro* website and courses have taught thousands the basics of engineering and production. His advice comes from Inner Circle Podcast #209.

Warren: When I was a kid there was a guy who told me, "Say yes, then figure out how you're going to do it afterwards."

That was the difference between me living in England and maybe teaching guitar for a living, and living in the hills of Los Angeles with a studio in my house making records with people I admire.

> *"Say yes, then figure out how you're going to do it afterwards."*

It's a big differentiator, because if you sit me down and ask me what I think of myself I'll tell you that I'm just some kid who plays a bit of guitar and likes making music.

That's what I really think even though I've had thousands and thousands of hours of making records with The Fray or Aerosmith or James Blount. I've worked with all these great people, but I still think I'm just this kid.

If I relied on that and still thought like this outsider still trying to break in, I would never be anywhere. I'd never be successful or never have this career that I have.

So the whole idea of "Say yes and figure it out afterwards" means to just go for it. There's a little scared kid inside all of us, so just go for it!

———

Persistence Is The Key

#20: David Campos

David Campos has produced gold and platinum albums, won a Clio award for one of his jingles, and composed music for MTV, SABC and many more. His jingle clients have included Coca Cola, Hyundi, Krups, McDonalds, Toyota, and FIFA world cup soccer, among many others. He's also the creator of *Advanced Music Production*, one of the biggest online music production education platforms on the internet today. His advice comes from Inner Circle Podcast #210.

David: I would say that persistence is the key to everything in life. I used to think that it was secret knowledge, then I thought that it was genius IQ or talent, then I thought that it was networking and knowing the right people. All of those things are important, but what I've found is that persistence is the key because failing is a part of life.

My first 100 songs never saw the light of day. I've been successful at a lot of things in the business, but every one of those things was an absolute uphill struggle with problem after problem after problem.

> *... persistence is the key because failing*
> *is a part of life.*

You've got to learn to be tough. You've got to learn to just push through. To me it makes no difference if I'm trying to solve a recording problem, or I'm trying to solve a Paypal problem in my online business, it's all about pushing through those challenges.

Whenever you overcome a problem, just think of all the guys on the side of you who didn't overcome that problem. That's when they get left behind and when you push forward.

All the successful people that I know in the music business, they've all got that trait. They're all tough people. The weak people, the lazy people that feel sorry for themselves, they fall by the wayside and then I make it.

———

Plan On It Working

#21: Dave Hampton

Dave Hampton has been an audio engineer for more than 20 years, working in a variety of capacities, both in the studio and on the road for clients that have included Prince, Herbie Hancock, Marcus Miller, RZA, M.I.A. and many others. Dave also writes about the music business, authoring two books about how to build a career as an audio engineer. His advice comes from Inner Circle Podcast #57.

Dave: Herbie [Hancock] gave me one lesson that was really good, and that was he would like to experiment with a lot of new things. My fear as a technical person was that the thing wouldn't work or would break at some point because we were using it at such a young stage of its development, so I would always have a plan B available when we were going to use something that was new.

> *"Commit to what you're doing and it will work out."*

We were going to do a keynote speech for AES, and I had this intricate plan that I'd worked up because we were using an early version of Logic during the demonstration that hadn't been released yet (they were rewriting it every night for us). I had all this intricate stuff worked out, and probably about the third revision of software Herbie said to me, "Dave, why don't you just plan on it working."

At that point I put all my plan B's away and I just focused on supporting what was going to happen with it all working, and he was right - everything worked.

Ever since then I don't put all that energy into that secondary plan. He was telling me, "Commit to what you're doing and it will work out," so I learned a valuable lesson there.

2

Learn To Network

Regardless of how much talent you may have, unless someone hears about what you're doing you'll end up creating in your bedroom your whole life. One of the keys to getting ahead for many of us is through personal networking. While this comes easy and natural for some, others find it unbelievably difficult, but you might not find it so challenging after reading this chapter.

Never Burn A Bridge

#22: Dae Bogan

Social media expert Dae Bogan is the co-founder and CEO of TuneRegistry, and currently serves as an Innovation Fellow at the UCLA Center for Music Innovation as well as an adjunct professor at the UCLA Herb Alpert School of Music, CSUN Music Industry Administration, and SAE Institute Los Angeles where he teaches music business. His advice comes from Inner Circle Podcast #20.

Dae: The biggest thing that I've learned is to never burn a bridge. Networking is the #1 thing in this business.

People can be talented but not have the connections, or they can have the connections but not have the depth of a relationship. Networking will take you a very long way.

Networking is the #1 thing in this business.

——

Get Out Of The House

#23: Richard Gibbs

Film composer Richard Gibbs has had a notable career, from being a member of the Los Angeles cult band Oingo Boingo, to playing on hundreds of records as a session musician, to composing the music for television shows like *The Simpsons* and *Battlestar Galactica* and over 60 films. Not only that, Richard owns one of the most innovative studios on the planet (Woodshed Recording), ranking in my personal Top 5. His advice comes from Inner Circle Podcast #38.

Richard: One thing that I always say when I speak to young musicians is that if you're home, you're losing.

Never be home. Always be out of your house. If you're watching TV, you're done. You've got to get out of the house. It doesn't matter what you do, just get out and do things. It's like a shark - if you're not moving, you die.

...if you're home, you're losing.

———

Activity Breeds Activity

#24: Mike Gromely

We've met Mike previously in Advice Tip #9.

Mike: The motto of my company is "Activity Breeds Activity." If you do nothing, nothing is going to happen, but if you do something, then at least something will happen.

If you do nothing, nothing is going to happen, but if you do something, then at least something will happen.

I would take artists to parties and functions, and we'd leave and they'd say, "Why did we go there?" I would say, "I don't know, but I'll tell you when it happens."

If you're active you're going to come across somebody who's got something for you or believes in you. It happens all the time, so you have to keep on going and not give up. You may not reach your exact goal, but it will have a positive effect on you in some way.

———

Give Out Your Card

#25: Candace Stewart

Studio management is an art unto itself and every studio owner knows how difficult it is to find a good one. Candace Stewart is one of the best there is, having spent over 20 years managing some of the most noted facilities in Los Angeles. She's now the manager of the famous EastWest Studios in Hollywood (formerly Western Recorders and the home of the legendary engineer and audio inventor Bill Putnum). Her advice comes from Inner Circle Podcast #159.

Candace: Go to local shows, give out your card, and meet with the band after the show, especially if you're a studio owner or manager or engineer. I still do this with my runners.

I have them go to shows and bring me bands that they think are cool because you never know when there's going to be an open day or open week where you can get someone in at a good demo rate. For me it's about selling the time, but at the same time it's about them learning how to network and how to get business.

Don't be a snob and think that you only have to know the most famous artist managers and producers. Get down there on a grass roots level. Go to clubs and keep in touch with the music that's happening in your town. Give someone your card and say, "I'm the studio manager. If you ever need any studio time just call me and come see the studio and I'll be happy to work with you."

Go to clubs and keep in touch with the music that's happening in your town.

You Have To See And Be Seen

#26: John Greenham

Mastering engineer John Greenham has won 3 Grammy awards and has been nominated for 6 others. His client list includes work for Katy Perry, Mary J Blige, Ice Cube, Jennifer Lopez, Sam Smith and many more. His advice comes from Inner Circle Podcast #187.

John: In this business what I've found is that you do have to go out and go to shows to meet people. You don't necessarily get work out of it but you do have to see and be seen.

> *I've found that if I stop going out, about two or three months later I'll stop working.*

I have a tendency not to do that, but I've found that if I stop going out, about two or three months later I'll stop working.

There seems to be some mysterious law of the universe that people will forget about you if you don't go out, but no one will criticize you for going out and handing out some business cards.

———

Most People Want To Help

#27: Chris SD

Chris SD is a music producer who's worked on 5 albums that have won Juno Awards (Canada's Grammy) among his 7 nominations, and was also nominated as Engineer Of The Year in 2012. Chris also teaches songwriters how to license their songs with his "The Art Of The Song Pitch" course. His advice comes from Inner Circle Podcast #199.

Chris: I had a friend who I met on a video shoot for an artist that I produced and he asked me to meet him at a club. He was from a different city, yet all of these people in the industry kept on coming up to him and saying, "Hey Mike. How you doing?" I looked at him and said, "How do all these people know you?" He wasn't a shmoozer or a gabby kind of guy. He's pretty unassuming and chill. He said, "I just go out. I go to everything that I'm invited to, or if I see something interesting I make sure to go. I meet people and get talking and all of a sudden I've got things going on."

I really took his advice to heart and started doing the same thing to expand my network, but without being "shmoozy" or having an agenda. It's amazing how well that works.

> *"I meet people and get talking and all of a sudden I've got things going on."*

To translate that to people who don't live in big cities, it works exactly the same online. Figure out who you'd like to have a relationship with and who you like the vibe of.

Don't be afraid to get yourself out there and drop people an email, and get on some forums and Facebook. Ask for an introduction from a friend. Just be you, be friendly, but be open. Most people are great people.

Although you might get the odd rejection, most people want to help other people because we're all in this together. You don't have to stick with the connections that you don't like. You don't have to like everyone and everyone doesn't have to like you.

Just hang out with the people that you think are cool and that think you're cool and you're going to be much more powerful as a group.

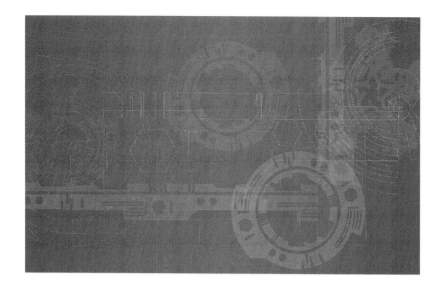

Play Well With Others

It's pretty much a fact of life that given a choice, people would always rather work with people that they like regardless of the talent involved.

Even more than talent, a pleasing personality goes a long way towards being successful not only in the music business, but any business. This chapter will provide many examples of that broad advice.

Don't Argue With Clients

#28: Jason Brennan

Warner Brothers supervising sound editor and re-recording mixer Jason Brennan is a one-man gang as he handles just about everything that has to do with audio on a TV show, from cutting dialog to recording music, ADR and effects, to mixing the shows. His advice comes from Inner Circle Podcast #19.

Jason: Be humble and don't argue with your clients. It's their vision, even if they're wrong. In reality, usually 95% of what you've done is actually staying as is, and they're not asking for it to be completely redone, so it's not a big deal.

This is ultimately what your job is - to give them what they want and with a smile.

...give them what they want and with a smile.

The Music Business Is About People

#29: Ross Hogarth

Ross Hogarth started in the business as a stage tech and live mixer for the likes of David Lindley, Jackson Browne and Fleetwood Mac, and eventually moved into the studio where he's since worked with music luminaries like Roger Waters, Motley Crue, Van Halen, John Mellencamp and many more. His advice comes from Inner Circle Podcast #41.

Ross: One piece of great advice was told to me recently when I was working with Van Halen. Alex (drummer Alex Van Halen) would constantly say, "You know, people are so misguided. They think that the music business is either about music or business. It's really about people." I realized that was something that I had learned early on but I never spoke it, but it's definitely a very important piece of advice that we miss sometimes.

If you want to be successful, you have to be able to interact and connect with people. In my job as an engineer and mixer and producer, if I can't read and understand people and then serve that, then I'm not going to be hitting the mark and I'll be unsuccessful.

That then circles back to everything technical as an engineer because you then step into the studio and you understand the person that you're working with. It's interesting that Alex would say that to me because I used every ounce of my people skills working with those guys because it was their first record with David Lee Roth in 20-some years and his interaction with Eddie and Al, and then Wolfie [Eddie's son] led my interactions with them. So it's really all about people.

If you want to be successful, you have to be able to interact and connect with people.

I knew and felt that way inherently but when it was told to me in that way then I could feel, "Your right, and now I can really understand that that's true."

I start from a very existential place. I believe that who you are is what you do. That creates a result and that's what you get. So the three words I always keep in order in my life is "Be, Do, Have." Who you are first is what you're being, and that creates what you do, and that creates what you have as a result. When those words get out of order, my life gets out of order. When Alex said that to me it really resonated, and I hear that conversation frequently in my head.

——

Have A Great Time While Working

#30: Richard Chycki

Richard Chycki is a multi-platinum engineer and mixer whose clients include such rock royalty as Rush, Aerosmith, Dream Theater, Mick Jagger, Alice Cooper and many more. His advice comes from Inner Circle Podcast #43.

Richard: The whole idea of having a great time and a great relationship with an artist is that you can hear it in the recordings. The best thing for me is when an artist talks about how much fun it was to do a project with me rather than the technical stuff. For me, that's the biggest compliment.

If they had a great time in the studio with you, that's how you get clients that stick with you for years. They know we're going to make a good record, but they also know that we're going to have fun doing it. We're making records for a living. How could life be any better?

If they had a great time doing it, that's how you get clients that stick with you for years.

If you're enjoying yourself while recording your album, that's going to make it to your record. Read the reviews that say, "The band sounds hot," or "The band sounds fresh," or "They sound young and alive."

These are all the things that manifest themselves because the band is having a good time. For me that's the biggest thing. Get the artist comfortable, have fun, and think about how fortunate you are to be able to make records.

———

Do Something For The Greater Good

#31: Richard Gibbs

We've met Richard before back in Advice Tip #25.

Richard: I see a lot of people coming into the business that seem to be asking, "What can you do for me? How much are you going to pay me? How is this going to help my career?" You're dead in the water if you think like that.

Your attitude has to be "How can I help you?" That has to be the first thing that you think whenever you meet somebody. "How can I help you?"

What improves the human endeavor overall is doing something for the greater good and doing something to make life a more pleasant existence, at least for somebody. That's certainly been my guiding light.

Your attitude has to be "How can I help you?"

—

Help Them Achieve Their Vision

#32: Bob Bullock

Nashville-based engineer Bob Bullock has worked with some top-shelf Grammy winners, including Steely Dan and Shania Twain, as well as Kenny Chesney, Jimmy Buffet, Reba McEntire and many more. His advice comes from Inner Circle Podcast #34.

Bob: I don't know that there's any real formula for success in the music business, but what I have seen from my decades in the industry and what has always mattered and kept me grounded is knowing that everybody that I have worked with, whether I was the assistant, engineer, or producer, was working on their dream.

It's the most important thing to them, which makes it the most important thing to me. That is the one thing that the people I learned from brought to the sessions.

If I can bring something that makes them happy and makes them feel that I've helped them achieve their vision, to me that's the most important thing.

No matter who I am working with, it doesn't matter whether it's a super star or someone doing a demo, it's always equally as important.

If I can bring something to the music production that makes them happy and makes them feel that I've helped them achieve their vision, to me that's the most important thing.

———

It's All About The Relationship

#33: Bob Brockman

"Bassy" Bob Brockman has a wide range of awards and credits, including more than 30 Grammy nominations with two wins, and an Oscar nomination. His many credits include Mary J. Blige, Toni Braxton, Brian McKnight, Faith Hill, Korn, Christina Aguilera, P Diddy, Santana, and Sting among many others. His advice comes from Inner Circle Podcast #28.

Bob: One thing that I've gotten from many people that I worked with is that it's all about your relationship with the people that you work with. It's not really about the record, it's not really about the song, it's about the people. I think Quincy [Jones] said, "You can spend two years working on a record and the label might not release it, so you better enjoy your time in the studio."

We all know it's a grueling business and it's really hard and on many projects you go for weeks on end with lack of sleep. People get burnt out and there's a lot of battle fatigue in the studio, so minding your relationship with the people you're working with is super important.

> *It's not really about the record, it's not really about the song, it's about the people.*

I also think that you have to figure out how to take care of yourself, whatever that might mean to you. For me it means more and more leaving the control room and going on walks because the studio can be such an obsessive enterprise that you really get lost in the sauce a lot and lose your way. Artists lose their way, mixers lose their way and producers lose their way all the time and lose confidence in what they're doing.

I can think of a lot of circumstances where I encouraged a producer I was working with, not because I was trying to grease him, but because I was trying to make him feel good about what was already there, even though he or she had lost their perspective. It's actually that kind of teamwork that is super important.

I don't know if there's enough emphasis on that in the educational system. There's such a strong emphasis on all of the technical aspects of the job, but it's really not a technical job. We all know this. Like the magic "producer fader" where you say, "Take this fader and ride it." It's sort of an inside joke, which you can't do in the box anymore [laughs] because everyone knows what's going on and is much more in tune with what's happening. They're scrutinizing what you're doing at every juncture.

You also can't bullshit as much as you used to, because they can just open up your automation and see what's going on.

Not that I'm trying to do that, but there was generally a lot of that historically because they weren't necessarily in touch with what was happening and were just listening what was coming out of the speakers. What was happening to the guts of the mix was the purview of the mixer and it's not any more, so it's more about acceptance and teamwork than it's ever been.

———

Service, Service, Service

#34: Ellis Sorkin

Studio Referral Service is the brainchild of Ellis Sorkin, who as a staff engineer for many years at A&M studios developed the concept of having a central booking agency for recording studios. In the 30+ years that S.R.S. has been around they have arranged studio time for Nirvana, Foo Fighters, Lady Gaga, Metallica, Pink, Katy Perry, Eminem, 50 Cent, Linkin' Park, Korn, Limp Bizkit, Red Hot Chili Peppers, and virtually every major music star you can think of. His advice comes from Inner Circle Podcast #48.

Ellis: I think from the engineering standpoint you should be humble and be seen but not necessarily heard, unless you're needed to be. Be efficient and perfect in what you do because there's no room for screw ups.

In the general studio business world, I think it's just service, service, service. Be available, be flexible, and be really good at what you do.

Be available, be flexible, and be really good at what you do.

———

Don't Take It Personally

#35: Elliot Scheiner

Elliot Scheiner is at the very top of the list of the most celebrated engineers with 8 Grammys (and 25 nominations) and 2 Emmys to back that up. From his very first hit (Van Morrison's *Moondance*) to the highest levels of music art and commerce mixing Steely Dan, The Eagles, Beyonce, Fleetwood Mac, Foo Fighters, Eric Clapton, Sting, and Paul McCartney (just to name a few), Elliot has been the man to go to when a superstar needs a hit. His advice comes from Inner Circle Podcast #51.

Elliot: I learned fairly early that most engineers take things personally. You get hired to do a project maybe by someone you don't know. They're hiring you maybe because of another record that you did. You spend some time doing what you do and the artist comes in and says, "No, I don't like this. This kinda sucks," and you take it personally. "This guy doesn't like what I do. What kind of bullshit is this?"

What I learned is that it's got nothing to do with that. An engineer has to remember that he's a hired gun and he's there to solve a problem, not to create one. So when someone comes in and doesn't like what you do, the response is, "How do you want me to change this? What are you looking for?" You want to try to achieve that rather than taking it personally and saying, "Get the fuck out of here."

> *They hire you because they like what you*
> *do. You just have to do what they need.*

That was probably the biggest thing in my life, but it's not your record when it comes down to it. It's not your name on the record, it's the artist's, and you've gotta make him or her happy. It's what they want to achieve or the producer wants to achieve and not what you think you bring to the table. You're just a soldier. You're a hired gun, and you have to achieve what they want.

I learned this early on in my career. I started getting a lot of work because of Van Morrison's *Moondance* record. I remember working with someone and they hated the drum sound and I took it really personally. I don't even remember who put the thought in my head that it wasn't about me, but somebody did and I'm thankful for that.

I tell that to people all the time. "You've got to be more open minded as an engineer. You may be used to doing one thing, but that may not work for everything." They hire you because they like what you do. You just have to do what they need.

―――

It's A People Business

#36: Michael Carnes

Michael Carnes created reverb products for Lexicon for 25 years before he decided to go out on his own and start Exponential Audio. He now builds a new generation of reverb and effects plugins that are widely used by professionals in every corner of the audio business. His advice comes from Inner Circle Podcast #53.

Michael: It's a people business. I make technology for a living and I'm glued to the computer far more than I should be (so is everyone else in the business) but this is really about talking to people. People aren't sold by specifications. They hear that stuff all day long but they don't care. What people in this business have are problems to solve.

If you're a producer, you've got to have people skills like nobody else. You've got to make a singer relax so that he or she can give you everything they've got and not feel like they're being held under a microscope. It's about making that person comfortable.

If you're in a position like me and you're trying to make a plugin that someone will use, then you ask questions. You talk to them about it and say, "What's hurting you? What's eating up all your time? What gets you yelled at?"

What people in this business have is problems to solve.

It's about knowing how to make people comfortable, and knowing how to solve problems. To do that, you just gotta talk to them. It's as simple as that.

———

Your Network Is Your Net Worth

#37: Mark Schulman

Mark Schulman has some amazing credits as the drummer for Pink, Cher, Foreigner, Cheryl Crow, and Destiny's Child, among many others. But that's not all. He's also a noted public speaker and author, focusing on leadership, team building and peak performance. His advice comes from Inner Circle Podcast #54.

Mark: I think it's a critical thing to me that your network is your net worth, because how you build you relationships, who you build your relationships with and how you nurture them, and how you are of service to people, determines your success.

Good business means that you're clear about what you want and you're clear about what you can offer, and you're clear about the tasks.

I've found that if I have desires or wants or needs or goals, I always try to give service to others inside those desires, wants, needs and goals, because I think that everybody benefits as a result.

Good business means that you're clear about what you want and you're clear about what you can offer, and you're clear about the tasks.

In good business, everybody wins, and everybody feels a sense of satisfaction and fulfillment from the negotiation. If you're dealing with any sort of business transaction and any of the parties feel less than satisfied, then it's not a satisfactory relationship.

———

It's A Business Decision To Be Nice

#38: John Jaszcz

Nashville engineer John Jaszcz, who's affectionately known in the industry as just "Yosh," has quite a history, recording the likes of George Clinton, Parliament Funkadelic, and Bootsy Collins in his native Detroit. His move to Nashville saw him record some of the greatest gospel and christian artists like Andre Crouch and Kirk Franklin, to country artists Billy Ray Cyrus and John Michael Montgomery. His advice comes from Inner Circle Podcast #59.

John: Be personable and don't be a dick [laughs]. You have to learn to be a fun person in the studio, and if you're good enough, you'll get some clients and they'll come back if you have a pleasant attitude.

Also, be nice to everyone, whether they're an intern or the president of the label, because as you know, that intern may become the president of the label one day.

> *Be nice to everyone, whether they're an*
> *intern or the president of the label,*
> *because as you know, that intern may*
> *become the president of the label one day.*

It will hurt you later if you're not nice to him, and I've seen that happen with some people, where they offended people early on in their career and then lose opportunities to work because the person they offended ends up being in a position to hurt their business.

So it's a business decision to be nice. You should generally be nice to people anyway, but it can hurt you in business if you're not.

———

Your Social Skills Have To Kick In

#39: Carmen Rizzo

Producer, artist, electronic musician, composer, DJ, remixer, and two-time Grammy nominee Carmen Rizzo has had a very eclectic career, from writing, engineering and doing the programming on Seal's classic album *Seal 2* to producing and writing for Paul Oakenfold's *Bunka* album, collaborating with Tuvan throat singers Huun Huur Tu, to co-founding the groundbreaking world music/electronic act Niyaz. His advice comes from Inner Circle Podcast #66.

Carmen: I think social skills are completely underrated and should be taken more seriously. I've spoken a lot at schools, and there's only one that I'm aware of that grades you on social skills which is Full Sail in Florida.

When you come out of school, hopefully you're pretty knowledgeable, but then your social skills have to kick in as does your skill set.

Over the years I've had many assistants and interns and that's where trust and social skills come in to play. I've had music celebrities like Chris Martin, Pete Townshend, Billy Corbin and Seal in my studio through the years. If I can't trust a person in that room if left alone, that can be a problem.

One example is I have had some interns who might not smell clean all the time, or there wearing flip flops and shorts every day, so if I take a client out for a meal somewhere nice, perhaps the assistant is not dressed to come along. It is important your assistant snow represent you just a little.

...at the end of the day, everybody in the room is talented, but who do you want to be around all day?

Some interns might have a chip on their shoulder and have way too much swagger. At the end of the day, everybody in the room is talented, but who do you want to be around all day? Sometimes I have gotten gigs because maybe someone just likes me better but there might be more talented people out there not working, and maybe they just don't like that persons. The point is it is not all talent, you have to like the person as well.

Just Be Cool

#40: Rich Walters

Television and film composer Rich Walters has been nominated for 2 Emmys and and 2 Canadian Screen awards, with recent credits that include the Sci-Fi Network show *Olympus*, and the feature film *Chappie* (with Hans Zimmer). His advice comes from Inner Circle Podcast #68.

Rich: One of my mantras is to "just be cool." That's it. Don't overreact when you're asked to do something, just smile and be professional all the time. Don't let them see you sweat, be grateful, and just do it.

A friend of mine told me something a few years ago and it stuck with me ever since. It comes from my friend Lee Smith, who's a famous film editor.

He said, "When we take a job, at that point we have given up the right to bitch about it, because we had a choice not to take it. Since we took it, we just have to dig in and do it." That kid of mentality is where my head is at.

> *"When we take a job, at that point we have given up the right to bitch about it, because we had a choice not to take it."*

Just be cool. You're going get asked to do some dumb, stupid things by people (things that you don't agree with at all), but they're you're clients and you're doing their project.

It's not your project, and you have to keep that in mind and just grin and bear it and do what your clients want, then you'll have success.

———

Honesty Goes A Long Way

#41: Joe Chiccarelli

Joe Chiccarelli has a ton of great credits as an engineer and producer, including Spoon, My Morning Jacket, Morrissey, White Stripes, The Killers, The Shins, Elton John, Frank Zappa and many more. His advice comes from Inner Circle Podcast #75.

Joe: Number one, you have to do this because you love it and you want to be in this business for the long time.

Also, I think being honest with people goes a long way. Managers and A&R people keep coming back because they trust that you'll tell them the truth as you see it. I'd rather people know where I'm at instead of tap dancing around and being dishonest about something. Building relationships is about the best thing you can do.

Building relationships is about the best thing you can do.

I find my career has gone through five year cycles. You have some hits and then you work non-stop for five years, and then you don't have a hit for a year and you're back to working hard trying to get gigs. You have another hit and it builds back up again.

Maybe the style of music changes and the music that you like to make no longer commands the biggest budgets, but you have to weather that.

Times change and there are cycles of music, so you have to learn how to ride those waves.

———

Play Your Cards Close

#42: Rob Schnapf

If you like the music of Beck, you can thank producer Rob Schnapf for discovering him. Rob has also worked with the equally provocative Elliot Smith, The Vines, The Whigs, and Booker T. Jones, among many others. His advice comes from Inner Circle Podcast #85.

Rob: Someone once said to me, "It's a very small business, so don't be an asshole." It wasn't that I was being one, it was just his way of saying that it's a small business.

The business really is all about relationships and it's great when you have them and it hurts when you don't. When a band is hiring experienced management, they're hiring their relationships.

The business really is all about relationships and it's great when you have them and it hurts when you don't.

The other thing is, "Play your cards close" [laughs]. In playing your cards close what I mean is be comfortable in the awkward silence. I don't mean it in a manipulative way, just that you don't have to fill that empty space with information out of discomfort. Let "them" do that, and it's really interesting what you can learn.

I've learned things that were absolutely none of my business because people talk too much. All of a sudden you find out the political minefield of something. None of that stuff is stuff I like or care about. I like being creative, and I've tried hard to stay away from everything else.

———

Be Compassionate And Forgiving

#43: Paul ILL

Los Angeles studio bass player Paul ILL has played with some of the greatest artists ever, including Pink, Tina Turner, Gwen Stefani, Courtney Love, Bob Weir and many more. That said, he has plenty of thoughtful insights about being a studio musician in today's new music world. His advice comes from Inner Circle Podcast #91.

Paul: You have to maintain what I call "spiritual principles," which is basically to treat everyone the way you or your loved ones would want to be treated no matter what goes down.

That means that sometimes we have to be compassionate and forgiving of certain people.

...treat everyone the way you or your loved ones would want to be treated no matter what goes down.

———

You Have To Be Flexible

#44: Tim Latham

Grammy-winning engineer Tim Latham has worked with a wide variety of artists across many musical genres, including the Black Eyed Peas, Kid Rock, Lou Reed, Erykah Badu, De La Soul, A Tribe Called Quest, The Roots, Britney Spears and many more. Tim has also worked on a number of Broadway cast albums, including the major hit *Hamilton*. His advice comes from Inner Circle Podcast #142.

Tim: You really better be able to get along with people. I can remember assisting on sessions where the mixer would be insufferable, or the producer was cranky, so the band wasn't very happy either, and I'm trapped there as the guy on the very bottom of the totem pole.

I remember sitting there thinking, "Why would someone spend all this money to be trapped in a room to be miserable?" I could never figure it out.

You really better be able to get along with people.

Interestingly, I met someone on the golf course through a friend who was just introduced to me as John. My friend told me that John and he used to work in advertising together. As we were playing I'm thinking to myself, "That guy looks kind of familiar." It turns out that he was an actor, and the way he got into acting was that one of the people at his agency said to him, "John, you're really good at your job but you're not great with the clients. Would you be interested in taking some acting lessons to get you more comfortable around people." He was up for it, and he fell in love with acting. Even though he started in his 50s, he's gone on to have a successful acting career.

And that was something that I learned from Bob Power (my mentor engineer). It was never anything that was consciously said, but he was just a very lovable, affable guy that you just wanted to hang out with.

I'm not saying that you have to change your personality any, but you really better to get along with a lot of different people. You have to be flexible.

———

Always Have A Smile On Your Face

#45: Bill Smith

Bill Smith got a chance to do what most of us just dream about, and that's assist for some of the music engineering luminaries during his days as an assistant at Capitol Studios in Hollywood, including as the personal assistant to the great Al Schmitt. Bill has gone on to have a great engineering career himself, working with artists like Yes, Quincy Jones, John Fogerty, Natalie Cole, and many more, plus on a variety of films and television shows. His advice comes from Inner Circle Podcast #160.

Bill: Always have a smile on your face. Always be happy to be there. Attitude is everything. Attitude will make or break you. Attitude can give you a career and it can also destroy your career.

Be the positive guy in the room, the guy that other people want to be around. Exude positivity. Be thankful you're there that day and you've gotten the call.

Don't ever let any success begin to affect you to where you feel that you have a right to there. Everybody is replaceable. The minute you begin to lose sight of that is the minute that you begin getting replaced.

At the end of the day it's not about the gear, (everybody can set a compressor or use a DAW - granted, some more effectively than others), because it's not the equipment that ever gets anybody work. We're all dealing with the same tools. The only thing that separates us is our attitude at the end of the day.

Attitude can give you a career and it can destroy your career.

It's great to be able to derive satisfaction and happiness from your work, but your personal satisfaction is never as important as that of your client.

Remember that you are there to serve the dream and vision of another. It's not about you or your technical skills, because it's always about someone else.

Your Connections Are Golden

#46: Mark Frink

Mixing stage monitors may be the hardest job in show business in that you have to keep so many people happy at the same time. Mark Frink is so good at his job that he's been trusted by some of music's biggest celebrities, including Tony Bennett, The Three Tenors, the Zac Brown Band, and most recently, The Eagles. His advice comes from Inner Circle Podcast #177.

Mark: I'm always surprised at how truly small our business is. You might encounter someone briefly and then move on in your careers. Our industry is so small that there's a really good chance that the experience you have with an individual on one day at one gig or in one studio is going to come back years later and have an affect on your career in a way that you can't understand in the moment.

Years ago I did a show at a relatively small venue with Tony Bennett at a time in his career when he wasn't doing quite so well (it was right before his big MTV *Unplugged* album). I did the gig and had a good time at the show, and a month later I got a phone call from the road manager. He called to hire me and said, "Tony remembered you from that day. I guess we had a good show and of all the people we've worked with in the last year, for some reason you're the guy whose name he remembered. He asked me to call you and hire you."

So the advice is to treat all of your connections in the business as if they were golden, because they really will make a difference.

That came out of the blue, but things like that happen in this business all the time and you just never know. I'm working for The Eagles this summer. Everyone that I interviewed with for the job had a past connection with me for some gig that I had done years ago. It was not my resume that got me the job. It was these personal connections.

So the advice is to treat all of your connections in the business as if they were golden, because they really will make a difference. If you're not a performer, your job is to create a safe, comfortable environment for your artists to enjoy themselves, because as Tony Bennett used to say, "We don't get paid for the gigs - We get paid for the travel."

———

Support Your Friends

#47: Frank Wells

Frank Wells started his career in the music business as head of technical services at the famed Masterfonics studio complex in Nashville, but then made a left turn when he became editor first of Audio Media Magazine, and then later Pro Sound News. Frank is currently a marketing, content and technology consultant so he's able to see the big picture of the audio business as few can. His advice comes from Inner Circle Podcast #180.

Frank: There was this business consultant named Jeffrey Gitomer who used to speak at various audio conferences and one of the things that he said was, "All things being equal, you want to do business with your friends. All things being unequal, you still want to do business with your friends."

If I have resources to do a job and there are people needing such a job done, make friends first, then use your resources to support your friends. Success has followed that philosophy.

"All things being equal, you want to do business with your friends. All things being unequal, you still want to do business with your friends."

Reputations Go A Long Way

#48: J.J. Blair

Grammy-winning producer/engineer J.J. Blair has a wide variety of credits that go from Johnny Cash to Rod Stewart to Weezer to the Black Eyed Peas, and many more. His advice comes from Inner Circle Podcast #181.

J.J.: I don't know if what I have to say is business advice as much as it's how to be in the business, but there are two things - stay teachable and be kind.

Once you kind of get to the inner sanctum of the business, everybody knows each other and reputations go a long way. You've got to be a really successful hitmaker for people to put up with your bullshit these days.

Stay teachable, and be kind

People always want to work with good people, and they know who they are, so there's no reason to be shitty to people. Know your stuff, stay teachable, and put your 10,000 hours in.

————

Treat Everyone As If They're Important

#49: Daryl Friedman

Daryl Friedman is the chief government and member relations officer for the Recording Academy. Daryl joined the Recording Academy in 1997 and established the organization's Washington, D.C., office, where he created The Academy's GRAMMYs on the Hill initiatives. His advice comes from Inner Circle Podcast #184.

Daryl: I think about this a lot because in Washington the power dynamic shifts back and forth quite a bit. i think that the best business advice is to treat everybody with respect, treat everybody fairly, and treat everyone as if they're important.

I've seen that play out, especially in Washington, because someone who's an intern today can be a member of Congress in a few years, and it's literally not an exaggeration to say that.

...treat everybody with respect, treat everybody fairly, and treat everyone as if they're important.

I've known people who've started at the very bottom on staff and later run for Congress and won.

It's a good practice in general, but it's also a helpful practice because power dynamics do shift and people do remember if you were respectful and that you were concerned and cared about their issues as well as your own.

——

Make Someone's Job Easy

#50: Nicholas Mishko

Nicholas Mishko is an artist manager who brings a blend of old school wisdom to modern management. After a stint at ABKCO Music and Records in New York watching deals made for music by legacy artists like The Who and Rolling Stones, Nicholas was well armed for negotiating recording and publishing contracts. That's a skill that many managers don't have, and one that makes his services indispensable to young artists. His advice comes from Inner Circle Podcast #188.

Nicholas: The best piece of business advice was the very first year I started at ABKCO.

Their senior vice-president Joe Parker brought me to his office and told me, "I've been in this business for long time and the best piece of business advice that I can give you is that there are a lot of jerks in the business, so be that nice guy that gets results and everybody will want to work with you."

From there I instilled being very easy to work with, being dependable, and getting things done into my work ethic. That's gotten me really far.

"...there are a lot of jerks in the business, so be that nice guy that gets results and everybody will want to work with you."

There are a lot of people that want to be tough negotiators, but you don't need to do that. If you can make someone else's job easy, they're going to want to work with you again.

If there are five people in the room but you're the easiest to work with and you can get results, you're going to get picked every time.

———

Solve Someone's Problem

#51: Gebre Waddell

Gebre Waddell started in the music business as a mastering engineer at his Stonebridge Mastering in Memphis, but he's always been into computer programming since he was a kid. He eventually turned that into a real business as co-founder and CEO of plugin developer Soundways. Gebre is also an author of the *Complete Audio Mastering Handbook* as well as President of the Recording Academy Memphis Chapter. His advice comes from Inner Circle Podcast #195.

Gebre: There are two things that come to mind. The first is that there is nothing more valuable than relationships and those interactions that you have.

When I was in my 20's I wrote off industry conferences and events and didn't recognize the significance of that. Connecting to communities, and interacting with real people is so key to success.

... there is nothing more valuable than relationships and those interactions that you have.

For a business, I'd say just make sure that you're solving a problem for people. That can be easily missed.

In the industry I see a lot of technical indulgences and that's something to be avoided. Make sure that you're solving a real problem for people.

———

It's A Small Community

#52: Chris Boardman

Acknowledged for his work in film, TV, records and academia, Chris is a six time Emmy Award winner with 13 Emmy Nominations, and has been nominated for an Oscar. Chris also taught the graduate film composition program at the University of Miami for 6 years where he was twice been nominated by The University of Miami Graduate School for their "Mentor of the Year Award." His advice comes from Inner Circle Podcast #211.

Chris: Be honest because, even though we may be spread out across the globe, this is a very small community of people.

If you're not ethical, or you don't stand behind your words, or you're not honest in your dealings, it will come back to bite you in the butt. Now in the world that we live in with trolls and bots, you can get destroyed in a matter of seconds.

> *If you're not ethical, if you don't stand behind your words, if you're not honest in your dealings, it will come back to bite you in the butt.*

Once you lose your reputation, you're done. As painful as it might be sometimes, be straight ahead, be accountable for your actions and you will find your way.

You may not get every gig that you wish, but that part of it is out of your control.

———

The Goal Is The Next Ten Years

#53: Nick Peck

For the last 20 years Nick Peck has been a sound designer and audio director for interactive projects and games at Skywalker Sound, Activision, Lucasarts, and now Disney Publishing Worldwide. Nick runs the audio department at Disney that handles sound design, music composition, and dialog casting/recording/editing for a host of award-winning iOS apps for franchises including Wreck-It Ralph, Monsters, Inc., Finding Nemo, Mickey Mouse Clubhouse, Brave, Up, Toy Story, Cars, Cinderella, Tangled, and many more. His advice comes from Inner Circle Podcast #212.

Nick: When you are creating a business or career for yourself, your goal is not the next gig, it's the next ten years. The result is that I would much rather make less money on a gig and have them think that I was a nice person than go in and be bellicose or arrogant and not have someone want to work with me again.

Being a nice person, having your diplomatic hat on, and really being flexible for other people (customer service), that's what it's all about.

> *I would much rather make less money
> on a gig and have them think that I was
> a nice person, than go in and be
> bellicose or arrogant and not have
> someone want to work with me again.*

That's what gives you the repeat bookings. That's what gives you the ability for someone to want to give you a job in which they're going to see you every day for years.

Always treat everyone that you work with with respect. I have to be enough of an optimist that the people who are nasty and out there backstabbing, that eventually people see them for what they are.

They're not the ones that keep the happy long career, it's the nice people that do.

———

The Separator Is You

#54: Mike Rodriguez

Mike is a senior audio mixer at Trailer Park in Los Angeles where he has amassed an enormous credit list that includes audio mixing for more than 260 film, television and DVD commercials including 21 HBO television specials, and an additional 35 network and cable television series and specials. Mike is also the creator and host of the AudioNowcast, which began in 2006 and is believed to be the longest running audio-specific podcast on the air today. His advice comes from Inner Circle Podcast #214.

Mike: With the tools that we have today, the playing field is now pretty even. It used to take a really great ear and a lot of time and talent, but with the technology that's available today you can almost buy your way into the business with the right kind of plugins.

I'm not saying that you can buy talent, but you can definitely start buying more and more quality.

A perfect example is Ozone. It's never going to replace a really great mastering engineer, but it's going to make your music sound better if you're not a mastering engineer if you know how to finesse it.

You can break out from the rest of the pack if you develop your own style of how you work the room.

So if the playing field is pretty even, what's going to separate you from the rest of the pack? The separator is you as a person. If you know how to "work the room," then you'll be able to be employed because people want to work with people that they like.

What makes them like you? A lot of times clients are just looking for affirmation on their project. Now obviously they're looking for a good mix or recording, don't get me wrong, but a lot of times they just want someone that they can feel confident in.

If I have a client who has the confidence in me that when they leave it will be good, or great, or amazing, then they'll just keep coming back to me.

Some of that stuff is just how you are in the room and how you conduct yourself. For instance, a real big thing is to never say "no" to the client - just make them change their "yes."

That's a big deal, because if you fight with a client and they give up and do it your way, they see it as a battle that they lost and they'll resent you every time that project plays afterwards.

So you can break out from the rest of the pack if you develop your own style of how you work the room.

✦

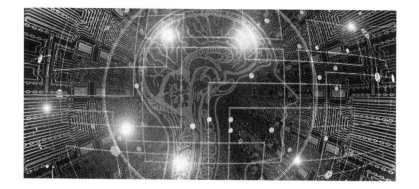

4

Educate Yourself

For most of us in the music business, the education never stops, and believe it or not, we're okay with that. Learning about new aspects of the business or new creative techniques should never ever get old, and you'll find that it never does to those that are successful. There's always something new to learn from those that have come before you, your current peers and contemporaries, and even from those just starting out in the business. Listen to what these mentors have to say about continuing your education both in business, marketing and creativity.

Understand The Engine

#55: Dae Bogan

Dae's words of wisdom can also be found in Advice Tip #22.

Dae: You should learn as much about the business as possible. You have to constantly educate yourself in this business because it changes all the time. It's not so much about learning the little nuances, but more about learning the specific philosophies behind how things work.

It's not so much about learning the little nuances, but more about learning the specific philosophies behind how things work.

You can measure a lot of things these days, but you have to understand how that metric translates to sales or capturing an audience. You have to understand the engine that's behind this new ecosystem within your segment of it.

Have The Largest Skill Set

#56: Wyn Davis

Best known for his work with the hard rock bands Dio, Dokken, Foreigner, Bad Company and Great White, engineer Wyn Davis style in that genre is as unmistakable as it is masterful. From his Total Access Recording studio in Redondo Beach, California, Wyn's work typifies old-school engineering coupled with the best of modern techniques. His advice comes from Inner Circle Podcast #40.

Wyn: From a studio and engineering standpoint, have the largest skill set that you can accumulate. In order to make a living in audio today you need to know how to do a lot of different stuff.

It's good to have a vocabulary of current technology and all the different kinds of music genres, and it's important to understand the post world because a lot of work that's available now comes from there.

The days of specializing as the guy who gets a great guitar sound is over. If you want to make a living or have a studio, you have to be able to do a lot of different things.

One of my most important clients right now is a voice-over client that does ads every week and it helps the continuing existence of the studio possible. The days of specializing as the guy who gets a great guitar sound is over. If you want to make a living or have a studio, you have to be able to do a lot of different things.

There's a lot of joy to be had in that we're doing something in our chosen field, but it's not always some star-studded event. If you love it, you'll be alright.

—

Learn To Love The Business

#57: Kellii Scott

We've heard from Kellii before in Advice Tip #7.

Kellii: Learn everything there is to know about it [the business]. Don't be lazy and expect someone else to do all the work for you. It's one thing to be a talented player, it's another thing to not know anything about what you're doing.

Ours is the only business where you can wake up and say, "I'm going to start this business of playing drums or playing music, but I'm not going to learn the marketing or PR or all those other things that are absolutely vital to success." You create the product and then you decide not to learn how to put it out into the world and be successful at it.

It's like a guy who makes clothes and opens up a store but advertise it. If you leave someone else in charge of everything, if it doesn't work out, it's always someone else's fault. When in reality it's never their fault, it's your fault because you made the choice to put the thing that you love most in life in their hands.

How are they supposed to make it successful? They will never love it as much as you do. It's like having a child and asking someone else to take care of it. That's just crazy. Why would you do that?

Learn everything there is to know about it [the business]. Don't be lazy and expect someone else to do all the work for you.

If you're going to learn and love to play you had better learn to love the business as well. Granted, maybe you'll never have the resources to become rich and famous, but that's not practical either. The ultimate goal is, "Can I pay my bills and live a life where I'm happy with the results of my work?"

The other reason is that the people that used to "take of everything" for the musician are out of business, so now the musician is forced to take on at least some of the work themselves.

I come from the old school where you gave all the work to someone else to take care of and frankly I did that because I was afraid and I was lazy and then we carry around the resentment that it was someone else's fault and therefore our dreams didn't come true.

Granted, maybe we didn't know any better, or the circumstances of the record business, the climate, the culture, and information was completely different then, but most of us were led to believe that that was the system that we had to work within and that's the way you're supposed to do it if you want to be successful.

I don't know if I ever met a musical entrepreneur back then that did it all themselves.

———

Don't Make A Decision Too Early

#58: Diego Stocco

Sound designer and composer Diego Stocco's not only worked on movies like *Takers* and *Sherlock Holmes*, television shows like *The Tudors* and *Moonlight,* and video games like *Assassin's Creed*, but he's also one of the people behind the great sounds on the Korg Z1 keyboard and Spectrasonics Atmosphere, Omnisphere and Trillian. His advice comes from Inner Circle Podcast #115.

Diego: I can say what helped me, when I was learning the basic skills, I wasn't necessarily learning how to become an engineer or performer. I didn't decide that I was going to become a certain type of professional. I just learned everything I could in every possible way.

I think that, number one, it kept me in business and working because I could switch from one thing to another without thinking that I wasn't fit for it, because I knew the skills. I did postproduction, commercials, jingles, playing with bands, dance music, and Pro Tools editing.

I was able to bring everything together, and I think that helped me a lot because now if I have an idea, I have the all tools to make it happen.

> *I just learned everything I could in every possible way. ..it kept me working because I could switch from one thing to another without thinking that I wasn't fit for it, because I knew the skills.*

So I would say to keep an eye open and don't make a decision too early in your life about what you want to become, because maybe you don't even know. Maybe you'll become something better.

———

Improve Your Craft Every Day

#59: Tony Shepperd

Engineer/producer Tony Shepperd has had an interesting journey in the music business that has taken him from Los Angeles to Nashville and back again. Along the way he's mixed projects for a variety of household names like Whitney Houston, Kenny Loggins, Barbra Streisand, Michael Jackson, Lionel Ritchie, and many more. His advice comes from Inner Circle Podcast #116.

Tony: I would say that the best advice is to just don't believe your own hype (laughs). It doesn't make a difference how good people SAY you are, you still have to constantly get better at your craft. I know a lot of guys, who at a certain point feel that they're at the top of their game and can't get any better, but each new day we HAVE to get better at our craft.

What we do is create art, and there's always a new way to stretch your artist palette and become better at the art that you're creating. Even if you're been doing the same thing for 15 or 20 years and it's been working, mix it up. Change it!

> *I would say that the best advice is to just don't believe your own hype (laughs)*

Most engineers have a sound and that's why people go to them. Don't get locked into that. Change your sound a bit because it keeps you fresh and it keeps you on your toes musically. You want people to say, "Wow, that's you, but it's you with a spin! That's really cool."

If you've been in "the box" all this time, put a piece of analog outboard gear into it. If you've been outside the box, try going just inside.

Learn to mix it up and push yourself so that you grow as an artist.

———

You Can Never Settle For Good

#60: Alex Benyon

Alex Benyon is a game audio designer and mastering engineer and has worked in a variety of positions on huge game titles like *Guitar Hero Live, DJ Hero* and *Call of Duty*, among many others. His advice comes from Inner Circle Podcast #122.

Alex: There's a constant learning curve and it's always evolving. You can't think that just because something was done a certain way for the last five years that's how we're going to do it now. You have to constantly evolve and try new things.

Audio is so important to video games, so you can never settle just for "good." Even if there are some amazingly crazy ideas, you have to try it. You have to keep pushing the audio and never let it get left behind by the technology.

There's a constant learning curve and it's always evolving.

Learn Music

#61: Tom Weir

Engineer Tom Weir is the owner of Studio City Sound, and has credits that include Rod Stewart, Blondie, Glen Campbell, Brian Setzer, Wille Nelson and many more. His advice comes from Inner Circle Podcast #126.

Tom: If you're going to get into the recording business, definitely learn music. I always tell interns that come in here to learn how to play the piano. If not the piano, then some kind of instrument. It's going to really help you later. You need some kind of musical knowledge more than just learning how to push some buttons. You have to know how to talk to your clients about music, and know about tuning and note manipulation. You've got to have an ear.

When I get a young musician in here, the first thing I ask is if they can play to a metronome. If not I tell them to get one on their phone right now.

> *You need some kind of musical knowledge more than just learning how to push some buttons.*

Otherwise, be as nice as you can be everywhere [laughs]. That can't hurt. No one's going to call you back if you're not good to work with.

___

Know Everything That Goes On

#62: Stevie Blacke

Stevie Blacke is a multi-instrumentalist known around Hollywood as the "strings guy" because he's often called upon to record full string sections of violin, viola, cello and double-bass (up to 40 tracks!) all by himself. He's played or recorded with a wide variety of music superstars, including Beck, P!nk, Madonna, Snoop Dog, Ludacris, Gary Clark Jr, Rihanna, Colbie Callait, and many more. His advice comes from Inner Circle Podcast #143.

Stevie: Livingston Taylor at Berklee [College of Music] told me, "If you're going to do this you should know everything that goes on. You should know the business side as well as the music side, otherwise you're going to get ripped off like so many other people have." So learn as much about the business as you can.

> *"You should know the business side as well as the music side, otherwise you're going to get ripped off like so many other people have."*

When I was in college I used to build stages in stadiums for concerts and do lighting for different bands coming through town, so I learned everything that goes on backstage hours and days before the show. A lot of musicians have no idea about that.

Discovery Excites People

#63: David Bock

After maintenance stints at such prestigious facilities as the Hit Factory in New York City and Ocean Way in Hollywood, Bock Audio Designs (formerly Soundelux) founder and managing director David Bock went from repairing vintage microphones to manufacturing them. David now utilizes his expertise to produce updated versions of the studio classics 251, U 47, U 47 FET, and U 67. His advice comes from Inner Circle Podcast #148.

David: The successful people that I've worked for and observed have always been open to learning.

One of the things that excites people most is discovery, whatever that may be. That's why people develop new hobbies and forget the old ones, because they've stopped discovering in that hobby.

The successful people that I've worked for and observed have always been open to learning.

———

Stay Up With The Technology

#64: Drew Drucker

If you were going to show someone how to make it in the music business, you'd point to engineer and mixer Drew Drucker as the perfect example. Drew graduated from recording school, then worked his way up in the business by starting as a runner and moving up the ladder thanks to hard work, paying his dues and taking advantage of some good timing. His client list now includes some of hip-hop and R&B's biggest stars including Wiz Khalifa, Juicy J, Travis Barker, Bruno Mars and B-Real, among many others. Drew's advice comes from Inner Circle Podcast #153.

Drew: Just never stop learning, first off. You always want to stay up with the technology and with everything that's new. I think Brian Eno said, "The technology is the sound of the generation."

If you listen to each decade, it changes with the technology, not with the people. The artists themselves move from decade to decade changing with the technology.

> *I think Brian Eno said, "The technology is the sound of the generation." If you listen to each decade, it changes with the technology, not with the people.*

Kanye West is a good example, where he started out making beats on MPCs and ASRs, and now he's implementing the latest technology.

Stay constantly learning, always be a student, and keep trying to stay on the forefront and push the envelope of what's currently happening. Try to create something new that will stand the test of time.

———

Learn From Unexpected Sources

#65: Bill Smith

We've met Bill previously in Advice Tip #45.

Bill: Always remember to keep learning, and remember that learning can come from unexpected sources. Things are always moving forward so you can't be wedded to what happened yesterday. Younger engineers have such a different approach, I'm always asking how they do things so I can incorporate it into what I do as well.

You want to garner new clients all the time, but after a while a lot of the new ones are younger than you are so you always have to be open to new ideas and new ways of thinking.

Things are always moving forward so you can't be wedded to what happened yesterday.

——

Operate In A Pro Environment

#66: Gary Noble

Engineer Gary Noble has won 3 Grammys and been nominated 18 times for his mixing and recording work. Gary's credits include Amy Winehouse, Jesse J, Nas, Josh Stone, Fugees, Wyclef Jon and many more. His advice comes from Inner Circle Podcast #168.

Gary: If you really want to do it, go for it. But here's the thing - regardless of what school you go to, when you graduate be prepared to be an intern even though you have the basic knowledge to work in a studio. I've met a number of people who just graduated and may know signal flow and Pro Tools, but they immediately expect to sit in the engineer's chair and start running the session. You may know more than the guy that just walked in off the street, but you still need to learn how to operate in a professional environment. Most of all, you need to know how to communicate and interact with clients.

When you work in a studio, whether you're on staff or free-lance, you're representing an organization. Throwing a tantrum because something doesn't work or there's a technical issue isn't a good look.

That aspect of it is a hands-on type of thing, so unless you're an intern in a studio while you go to school, that part still has to be worked on. You're dealing with different people, different personalities, different issues, and you have to remain very flexible. That's why I learned over the years that you have to be flexible as an individual and an engineer.

When you work in a studio, whether you're on staff or free-lance, you're representing an organization. Throwing a tantrum because something doesn't work or there's a technical issue isn't a good look.

Another thing is, when you're working with someone and they ask you for something, even if you think it isn't right, still try to give them what they want, because at the end of the day, it's their song. The music is a part of them. It's like a piece of their soul, so when you try to deny them what they're looking for, they take it personally.

You have to know how to walk that fine line between getting the job done to the best of your ability, and making them happy at the same time. That only comes with experience.

5

Own Your Content

Once upon a time it was rare for artists and songwriters to actually own the art that they were making. Today it's easier than ever to maintain control of your creative content, but you have to be aware not only of the possibilities that are available to you, but of its worth as well.

These mentors have been through the rigors of the business side of content creation, and their words can mean money in your pocket.

Your Online Accounts Are Like Masters

#67: Jay Coyle

Jay and Chandler Coyle formed Music Geek Services in 2009 to help artists and bands keep in touch with their fans, enlarge their audiences, and sell more merch. They've spearheaded new products, project management, and driven fan-focused initiatives for artists such as Veruca Salt, Barenaked Ladies, John Oates, and Jars of Clay among others. Their advice comes from Inner Circle Podcast #18.

Jay: When I started out as a consultant outside of the mainstream record business it was very much a DIY aesthetic. The idea was "Screw the labels. We don't need them any more."

You have to remember that there's been a big business built over time out there, and if you want to keep control of your vision, you can't do it all on your own. You need to find like-minded people to plug into.

... at some point you have to be mature enough to realize that you can't do everything on your own.

I've turned that around to, if you're a baby band, it's definitely "do it on your own and learn all the information that you can," but at some point you have to be mature enough to realize that you can't do everything on your own.

It's okay to ask for help and to plug into things, just as long as at the end of the day it's serving your career's goals.

———

#68: Chandler Coyle

Chandler: Always be helpful. Rather than being a taker, be a giver because it will always come back.

The other thing is to make sure you have control over all your assets. I don't mean about owning your masters, but to make sure that you know where your email list is, is it backed up? All the technical stuff, because if you can't log into your website because your web developer goes AWOL, you're out of luck.

...make sure you have control over all your assets. I don't mean about owning your masters, but to make sure that you know where your email list is, is it backed up?

We've seen a big artist lose control of their Facebook page. They spent years building up likes and then they lose control of it to a hacker. These are not just accounts, they're equivalent to your masters.

——

Never Give Away A Master

#69: Stonebridge

Stonebridge is one of the most musical and cutting edge electronic music producers on the scene today. He has been producing international hits since 1993 but most recently he's had some big ones with Ne-You, Britney Spears and Jason Derulo. He also hosts an acclaimed show on Sirius XM called *Epic Mix*. His advice comes from Inner Circle Podcast #21.

Stone: I never give away a master. A lot of young guys don't understand what a master is, but it's your pension. Be very careful with your masters and your publishing and get some advice before you sign anything, especially in this digital age. If you're sloppy you can let labels collect your royalties that you should be getting.

> *...at the end of your career you can control a catalog that can really be worth some money.*

License your songs, don't give them away. In the dance industry you can license for 5 years, and at the end of your career you can control a catalog that can really be worth some money.

Hold On To Your Publishing

#70: Martin Page

Martin Page has had much success over the years writing with everyone from Earth, Wind and Fire to Bernie Taupin to Hal David, to Robbie Robertson to Robbie Williams. He's also co-written a couple of world-wide #1 hits – "We Built This City" for Jefferson Starship and "These Dreams" for Heart. His advice comes from Inner Circle Podcast #113.

Martin: I think the best advice I've gotten as a songwriter came from my manager Diane Poncher when I first came to America, which was to hold on to your publishing rights. As we see on YouTube, people just post things up for nothing and think that it's so good to be heard and liked.

In the early days, to make my survival as a musician and to be able to buy my equipment, Diane said, "We want to get better percentages for you when we do publishing deals." All we want as artists is to be seen and get our music out there.

She made a point of taking notes of when these songs were released, so 30 years later we're able to pull back that publishing.

As a songwriter, owning the copyright of your songs is ultimately what you want. That is your lifeblood. Even if you have to sacrifice early on to give away your limbs and your fingernails and your hair [laughs], ultimately you're hoping that it's going to come back to you.

...songs are real things. Music is in the air, but the copyright when you write the song and when it's put down to paper and recorded, that is your own work that you hopefully will have a good percentage of for the rest of your life.

That's what I learned quite strongly from just being a naive kid. When I came across great managers I began to learn that a songwriter needs control of his copyright and not to give away his soul for having great work.

Early on when I came to LA, you'd write a song for a big band and they'd say, "We're going to take all the songwriting royalties. You can have the credit, but we're going to take all the money because we're a big band." And even in those days, although I wanted to break through, I just felt that it wasn't fair.

So the best information I got was that songs are real things. Music is in the air, but the copyright when you write the song and when it's put down to paper and recorded, that is your own work that you hopefully will have a good percentage of for the rest of your life.

That's the biggest thing that I learned and it put me in good stead for a lot of the years of my life.

6

Getting Paid

Making money for doing something that you love can be one of the most baffling parts of the business for someone starting out. Likewise, knowing how to price your content or your services can be equaling as confusing even for those who've been in the business for a while.

These words of wisdom may open a door to how the pros do it and how you can apply their techniques to your world.

Know Who You Work With

#71: Barry Rudolph

You may know Barry Rudolph from his many gear reviews in Mix and Music Connection magazines, but he's been an A-list engineer in Los Angeles for a long time as well. His credits include Rod Stewart, Lynyrd Skynyrd, Hall and Oates, The Corrs, Enrique Iglesias, Waylon Jennings, Johnny Mathis, Mick Jagger, The Beach Boys, and many more. His advice comes from Inner Circle Podcast #31.

Barry: Getting paid is the short answer. Know who you work with and that stuff takes care of itself. If you work with flakey people then you're going to have those kinds of things happen [trouble collecting money].

If you work with flakey people then you're going to have those kinds of things happen [trouble collecting money].

The other thing is to save money. You're self-employed so you have to worry about all the things you read about that go on with self-employed people. My motto early on was to have multiple streams of income, not just from engineering. In the 70s when it was slow in the studio I used to buy and flip houses.

Don't Chase Money

#72: Richard Gibbs

Richard appeared earlier in Advice Tips #25 and #33.

Richard: One piece of advice came too late for me. I wish I had heard it when I was younger. It came from Kobe Bryant, of all people. I heard him on an interview one day about negotiating his contract and he said, "Don't chase money; let money chase you."

I love that, and I wish I had known that back in the day when I was a kid and money is rearing its head.

More often than not you make the wrong decision if you're basing it on money...

More often than not you make the wrong decision if you're basing it on money, and I did, time and time again. There are many career choices that I wish I could take back because I did something for the money instead of for the love of it.

———

Give Your Work Value

#73: Andrew Scheps

Andrew Scheps has a long list of great mixing credits, from the Red Hot Chili Peppers to Adele to Metallica to Justin Timberlake and many more. He's also one of uber-producer Rick Rubin's go-to mixers. His advice comes from Inner Circle Podcast #39.

Andrew: I think the best thing I've done is to be terrified of not having enough money to live and eat and that kind of stuff (laughs), so I've been frugal. I do have a ton of gear, but 99% of it is old stuff that doesn't go down in value because I feel that if I don't ever work again I can at least sell it.

I guess another thing is the realization that there isn't free money out there, especially in the music business. There are so many bands that talk about the realities of dealing with a label, no matter if it's a major or tiny label, and have a lot of stories that are negative. They'll say, "I don't want to give up 88% of my income for what I'm going to get back, but as soon as somebody from any label larger than the one they have shows up courting them, they're falling all over themselves trying to get signed by them.

> *You have to be realistic about commerce while you're doing the art, while setting yourself goals that are reachable.*

Getting signed is still this magic thing. I think it's important to stay realistic as much as you can, because the music business is basically worse odds than the lottery at this point. But it's still the lottery and you can still have some massive success. You have to be realistic about commerce while you're doing the art, while setting yourself goals that are reachable. Try to assess things properly and don't get carried away by the concept of it.

For engineers, you need to give your work value, and it's really hard to give it away then go back and say, "Yeah, but I'm worth a bunch of money." So many people say, "Oh, but you love your job."

Yeah, but it's still really hard work and even if it were easy, I still need to eat. So either nobody in the business should get paid because it's all for the art, or it's okay for us to want to get paid? There's a real disconnect about that.

And also, there are so many myths about bands making money playing live. Almost everyone loses money on their tours. It's a little better now that gas prices have gone down again, but you cannot make money on tour unless you're playing arenas.

Plus it costs an unbelievable amount of money to be an opening act on a big tour, so this myth of bands getting rich driving around in vans is crazy. It's good for people not to think that's true either.

———

It's A COD World

#74: Dennis Moody

Dennis Moody has become the "drummer's engineer," with all-star drummers Dave Weckl, Steve Gadd, and Michael White as regular clients. As a live concert engineer, Dennis has mixed everywhere from Carnegie Hall to Madison Square Garden and most of the major concert venues throughout the United States and Europe. His advice comes from Inner Circle Podcast #50.

Dennis: Business-wise, I like working for independent companies. Before I used to work for a lot of major record labels and I used to chase the big artists and try to get involved with those big label deals. It used to be 30 day billing. Now it seems to be 180 days and they want to renegotiate your bill after the fact. The smaller companies not so much.

So I dropped my rate down a little bit as long as it's COD (collect on   delivery) and I've had no problems getting paid since then, and I have more work than ever.

> *I dropped my rate down a little bit as long as it's COD and I've had no problems getting paid since then.*

Some Money Costs Too Much To Make

#75: Dave Hampton

We've met Dave before in Advice Tip #21.

Dave: I learned another one is that some kinds of money cost too much to make. That's one that I pass on to a lot of people because a lot of times you have to measure how you give of yourself in the situation.

When I started I would do anything because it was work and I loved what I was doing, but I'm well into this, so I do something now because I choose to and it's an investment past money.

You invest in people and you invest in situations. I'm not a young guy anymore and it's a young man's game, but I have a full appreciation and my one desire is to, as the comic books say, "Use my super powers for good." [laughs]

If I do that, more and more people will be able to play their instruments live and be able to make a living in this business.

When I started I would do anything because it was work and I loved what I was doing, but I'm well into this, so I do something now because I choose to and it's an investment past money. You invest in people and you invest in situations.

—

Know Your Value

#76: Rob Arbitteir

Music technologist Rob Arbitier is not only one of my compadres from the AudioNowcast podcast, but he's been Stevie Wonder's technology guy for 30 years, as well as a composer/producer for commercials, movie trailers and albums. His credits include commercials for Nike, Kodak, Old Navy, Hot Pockets and Coke, and trailers for major motion pictures. His advice comes from Inner Circle Podcast #65.

Rob: Probably the biggest single piece of advice is to know your value. Understand your worth even from the beginning. When I started with Stevie Wonder, what I did back then had real value and he realized it, but I didn't. We worked it out as the years went on, but you have to understand that even if you're just starting out, if you have something unique to offer (and it could be technology or musical creativity or anything else), even on your first day, you have some real value.

The Hot Pockets commercial jingle that I did is a good example. Sure, my production partner and I did it for very little money because we were just starting out and thought we had to, but we were creating a sound signature for a brand that was going to help launch it into a multi-billion dollar company. I had no sense of it back then.

I clearly understand now what we were doing and how they were kind of taking advantage of us, although they were a small company at the time too. Understand your value. Don't be so quick to do things for a buyout. You may be helping build a brand that's going to be worth a lot of money down the road.

...if you have something unique to offer (and it could be technology or musical creativity or anything else), even on your first day you have some real value.

In the case of Stevie, I was creating something for him that was going to revolutionize his way of working and thinking. It's not that he didn't appreciate it, because he did, but I was just so focused on the fact that I was getting to meet my musical hero that I didn't think of the business aspect of it. So even if you're doing things that you feel you're lucky to be doing and it's benefiting you, understand that you're benefiting the other party as well.

Don't sell yourself short, even from the very beginning.

Don't Base Your Career On Money

#77: Carmen Rizzo

Carmen was previously quoted in Advice Tip #39.

Carmen: Base your career not on money, but on the music that you make.

No one checks your bank account or asks you how much money you made on a project. They say, "You were part of that project?"

Don't base your career on money but on the music that you make. No one checks your bank account or asks you how much money you made on a project.

That's something that you need to hang you're hat on. The work that I'm the most proud of has never been the highest paying.

—

Get Your Money First

#78: Bob Hodas

Bob Hodas has been tuning studios for over 20 years for clients like mixer Dave Pensado, producer Tricky Stewart, composer Danny Elfman, and recording artist Stevie Wonder, as well as major recording and film studios all over the world. His advice comes from Inner Circle Podcast #71.

Bob: Chris Stone [the founder of the famous Record Plant recording studios] taught me to get your money before you release the product. That probably was the best advice he could give me [laughs].

I hate to say it, but there came a point in my career where I had to stop billing people. Regrettably, some people stop paying their bills. Chris would say, "Once they have the tape, they have no incentive to pay."

...get your money before you release the product. Chris [Stone] would say, "Once they have the tape, they have no incentive to pay."

Save Your Money

#79: Gary Solt

You've met Gary previously in Advice Tip #4.

Gary: My advice to people first starting out is to save your money. If you're on something that works out and you get some money for it, always put some of it aside, because you never know if that's going to be the last gig you get. If you think that the taps have just been turned on and they're never going to close, you're a fool.

Save your money, invest your money, and always live below your means, then as a business person, you'll be successful. It's true and it's common sense.

> *If you're on something that works out and you get some money for it, always put some of it aside, because you never know if that's going to be the last gig you get.*

——

Trust Your Instincts

#80: Walter Turbitt

Walter Turbitt is a gifted producer, engineer and musician, but now he's ventured into management and is working with DJs and EDM artists. His advice comes from Inner Circle Podcast #90.

Walter: There's a balance between protecting yourself and trusting who you're working with.

I find that there are some people that are afraid to send out a song that they want you to work on because they think you're going to steal it. Yes, you have to protect your interests because publishing still has a value, but you still have to be able to trust someone and even gamble a bit.

There's a balance between protecting yourself and trusting who you're working with.

You've got to be willing to pay your dues and do shows for nothing.

I work with artists that get up to $50,000 a night sometimes but I'll still do a show for free if it's the right business decision and we get some value for it.

There's a culture among many younger people that they're so concerned about getting screwed that nothing happens as a result.

Once piece of advice that I can guarantee is that if you don't do anything, nothing will happen. It's a simple saying, but it's totally true.

The other thing is to trust your instincts. At the end of the day you can sleep better at night, you like yourself when you look in the mirror, and you learn from it when it doesn't go your way.

———

Save For The Future

#81: Ken Caillat

Regardless of your age, you've no doubt heard much of the great Fleetwood Mac album *Rumors* over the years. The songs from that record are still played everywhere today, a tribute to the contributions to the project (as well as three other albums by Fleetwood Mac) by producer/engineer Ken Caillat. Ken has a long list superstar credits including The Beach Boys, Frank Sinatra, Pat Benetar, Herbie Hancock and many more. He's also the father and producer of singer/songwriter Colby Caillat. His advice comes from Inner Circle Podcast #103.

Ken: The thing I tell musicians is, "The music business is a rough business to grow old in, so if you're gonna do it, you'd better think about getting a 401k and be diligent about your savings."

There are a lot of people who had a lot of fun. A lot of studio managers I know, girls and women that were the managers and don't have a 401k and don't have a retirement plan. Or roadies I see all the time and they're sitting there struggling for money.

So to me, if you're gonna be in the music business, you'd better develop a 401k and save for the future.

---

*The music business is a rough business
to grow old in, so if you're gonna do it,
you'd better think about getting a 401k
and be diligent about your savings.*

You'll have to learn to be your own manager or hire someone to stay on top of your financial plan for you.

———

Know Your Worth

#82: John Kurzweg

If you've listened to rock radio, you're certainly familiar with producer/engineer/musician John Kurzweg's work, as he's produced twelve #1 singles and another eight top 10's for bands like Creed, Puddle of Mud, Godsmack and many others. John's led a really interesting musical life, from an early guitar teacher telling him to give up, to a career as a solo artist, to engineering hits in his living room. His advice comes from Inner Circle Podcast #105.

John: That is a great question and a very hard one for me in that I don't consider myself a very good business person. What comes to me in this moment (I might answer it differently tomorrow) would be to know your worth. T

here's a lot of ego in the industry and certainly I've had my dose of that. I've been told in the past that I didn't know my worth or what I was good at, and what I wasn't good at.

Certainly having a good attorney (and or manager) can help you know what you're giving up, what you're getting, and what to look out for.

I've always trusted that if I did good work I'm going to be taken care of and things are going to go okay. It doesn't always work out that way, but I think mostly it has for me, or at least 50% of the time [laughs], but I'm not always the wisest when it comes to business stuff.

I've been told in the past that I didn't know my worth or what I was good at, and what I wasn't good at. Certainly having a good attorney is going to help you there.

There's definitely a part of me that wants to walk out of the room and turn off when business begins. I'm so not interested in that. It's hard for me to stay engaged in the process and be an adult and make sure that everyone (especially myself) gets taken care of. It's grown-up stuff and it's hard.

———

You Can't Live On Free

#83: Bobby Summerfield

Bobby Summerfield has worked with a variety of great artists ranging from Michael Jackson to Carole King to world music superstar Johnny Clegg to the legendary Harry Belafonte. He's also a composer with his own music library, and his credits include shows like *Oprah Winfrey, The View, Survivor*, and ABC's *20/20 News*, and commercials for Coca Cola, Ford Motor Co. and American Airlines. Along the way, Bobby's also been nominated for a daytime Emmy award. His advice comes from Inner Circle Podcast #118.

Bobby: When people say the "music business" you must remember that it's 10% music and 90% business. It's the sad truth. So many of my mates are brilliant artists and talented people, but I often collaborate with them on television deals and I tell them that we're going to get a "sync." They then ask, "What's a sync?"

You really have to know the terminology. It's not hard to learn. You really must understand where you earn money as a writer or producer, who's making money, who's on your side, and who's against you. You really have to understand that.

You also really have to understand that as a new artist you're going to have to get reamed a little bit the first time around. Don't be greedy on your first deal. You're going to have to give away a bigger piece of the pie the first time, so just make sure that the piece doesn't last for the rest of your life.

Be smart. Get legal advice. Get advice from well-informed friends and from an attorney.

Generally the artists and everyone on the creative side of the fence are pretty fair people, but when it comes to royalties and money, people get quite nasty. The people that are smart understand that.

Get the business under control first, then learn your chops.

For instance, I get together and write songs with some friends, so it's the three of us in a room. The idea is that we're going to split it even three ways, irrespective if I got drunk and fell asleep on the couch, I get still a third because I'm snoring and it put you in a mood to write that song [laughs]. It's the easiest way to stay out of trouble.

We all know history, and for the most part, all the big bands that we knew were all full of peace and love coming up, but five years later began to hate each other as they sue each other over who wrote different pieces of the song. Get the business under control first, then learn your chops. Really, just understand it. It's not hard to learn.

Everybody can work for free, and everybody wants to be loved, but you can't live on love and freeness.

———

Don't Be Afraid To Monetize Yourself

#84: Vance Powell

Vance Powell is one of the few engineers to make a successful transition from live sound to the studio. After serving as the chief engineer at Nashville's acclaimed Blackbird Studios, Vance stepped out on his own with a string of Grammy awards from his work with Jars of Clay, Buddy Guy, Chris Stapleton and The Raconteurs. Since then Vance has been hot as both an engineer and producer, working at his own Sputnik Sound with Jack White, Arctic Monkey's, Willie Nelson and Neil Young, among many others. His advice comes from Inner Circle Podcast #166.

Vance: The best piece of advice I was ever given was from Richard Dodd. He said to me, "Don't be afraid to monetize yourself." The first thing he said was this though - "Don't ever do anything for free because if you do, whatever you do is worth nothing." That goes for doing things for friends, doing things for a band that you like - it's worth nothing to them because they paid nothing for it. Don't be afraid to monetize yourself. Don't be afraid to say what you think you're worth.

Even if you not worth that much, the market will correct you [laughs]. You'll suddenly price yourself out of work.

"Don't ever do anything for free because if you do, whatever you do is worth nothing."

By the same token, if you price yourself high, people love telling other people how expensive you are. They love saying, "I care about this record so much that I paid X thousands of dollars to mix it. And they love feeling like they've paid their own hard-earned money to get the thing that they want. Especially if you deliver it and blow them away, it's worth every penny to them.

I spent years managing myself, and I left so much money on the table because I would feel bad about pricing myself. The worst feeling in the world is when you say, "It's going to be X thousand dollars," and they immediately go, "Great!" Then you think, "I should have charged X times 2 thousand" because you know you're leaving money on the table.

That being said, sometimes karma is a crazy little thing. You never know when that thing you did for that guy that no one knew could turn into something really awesome.

Know When It's Time For A Loss Leader

#85: Dennis Dreith

Composer/arranger Dennis Dreith started in the business playing sax for The Beach Boys but soon turned to composing and orchestrating for commercials, television and motion pictures. Along the way he wrote the scores for cartoons, television movies, and motion pictures. Dennis also served as the International President of the Recording Musicians' Association for 15 years, and also was a consultant and member of the American Federation of Musicians Negotiating Committee. His advice comes from Inner Circle Podcast #182.

Dennis: There are two extremes and the best business advice is to balance them. You don't want to do things for free and be taken advantage of, but sometimes it's appropriate to approach your career like a business and know when it's time to have a bit of a loss leader.

...whatever the deal you made, is the deal you made, and you still have to give 110% if it's the biggest budget project in the world or it's the tiniest little budget and you feel like you practically gave it away.

There are times when it is entirely appropriate to give a young or upcoming producer working on a tight budget a break in price to help make a project happen especially if it means putting more value into a project. Think of it as an investment in your career and the Producer's. This, however, should be offset with something additional for you – a piece of the project, commitment of future employment, etc.

The other piece of advice is whatever the deal you made, is the deal you made, and you still have to give 110% if it's the biggest budget project in the world or it's the tiniest little budget and you feel like you practically gave it away. Whatever the project is, you treat it like it's the most important project in the world. You never know where that project is going to wind up and your performance always has to be the best you can make it.

———

Try To Be The Best

#86: Rich Tozzoli

Television composer and author Rich Tozzoli has written an incredible 16,000 music cues that have been used on more than 10,000 cue sheets on 714 television series! Rich is not only a great composer but he's also a talented engineer and the author of several books, including the *The Ultimate Guitar Tone Handbook* that we wrote together. He also regularly writes for a number of pro audio and guitar magazines like Pro Sound News and Premier Guitar. His advice comes from Inner Circle Podcast #183.

Rich: I love business and I will not be shy in telling you that I love to make money. However, I love to make money doing a craft and I feel strongly that I should be compensated for my work.

I was very lucky to go to business school in college and I've always loved to make money by doing art and by doing what I love. That's not a cocky statement that's just confidence in my product. Here's my product and this is what it's worth. So my advice to someone is to get so good at your craft that you can create your own financial destiny.

Those may be generic words but when you're a kid coming up the chain and you want to make money in this business - you know what? Are you better at Pro Tools than everybody else? Because if you are, you're going to make money. Are you better than your competitors at what you do?

You don't have to be the absolute best, but you have to get exceptionally good at your craft. Study it like nobody's business and that's the key. It's simple but it's absolutely true.

Also, specialize in something that your gut tells you to specialize in. When I was mixing surround sound my gut told me to specialize in that. With that in mind, I'm very much in favor of reading the tea leaves to where the financial implications of that particular aspect of business will go.

I could clearly see that surround sound was not going to pay me what I wanted and what I thought I was worth, so I evolved into television where royalties were a better way to go. It also allowed me to work on my own without too much supervision.

...specialize in something that your gut tells you to specialize in.

The point I'm getting at is for people just coming up in the business, unfortunately or fortunately depending how you look at it, you have to do everything to see what floats your boat and what will make you money while you float that boat. You have to look ahead one, three, five and ten years and say, "Is this going to be paying me enough money?"

Follow your instinct at what you think you're good at, and what you think you can be one of the best in the business at. That's a broad statement, but it really is true.

I tend to surround myself with literally the best of the best at what they do, and that's why you get great results.

———

Have Faith And Work Hard

#87: Jeri Palumbo

Jeri Palumbo is a television broadcast engineer, audio mixer and RF tech who's worked on hi-profile sports shows for more than 25 years. She's been part of the TV audio team for all of the most celebrated sporting events, including the Super Bowl, NBA and NHL playoffs and the Major League Baseball World Series. Her advice comes from Inner Circle Podcast #189.

Jeri: First of all, if you're a free-lancer it's really important to get a good accountant that understands the business and your write-offs and can help you navigate that. Then, set up some kind of retirement account that you put the money in yourself. Always squirrel some money away while you're working because you will be rabidly busy and then you'll have a slow season where the phone doesn't ring as much.

I think that every free-lancer freaks out when this happens. "Oh God, I'm never going to work again!" but then it ramps back up again and you may be busier than you've ever been. If you've put some money away you can cruise when it gets slow, because it will always ramp up and down.

Go where you are celebrated, not where you are tolerated.

Have faith, work hard and learn everything you can about your business. And this is a big one, I've always worked around truly amazing people, but not everyone is going to like you.

If you get into a group of people that just don't want to see you succeed, I believe that it's in your best interest to find your path that suits you. *Go where you are celebrated, not where you are tolerated.*

I really believe that if somebody doesn't want you to succeed there, you won't. That's not the place for you. Find the place where people celebrate what you're bringing to the table and you will always flourish.

—

Collect The Pennies

#88: Clarence Jey

Producer, songwriter, multi-instrumentalist and composer Clarence Jey,'s credits include music on US Billboard Hot 100, a Grammy-winning record, one of the largest viral music successes in history, and music for film and multiple Emmy-nominated TV shows. His broad musical spectrum ranges from creating music for the Grammy winning R 'n B group All-4-One, to the huge viral hit song "Friday," and music for *Glee, America's Best Dance Crew, America's Got Talent* and TV host Jimmy Fallon's Grammy-winning album *Blow Your Pants Off*. His advice comes from Inner Circle Podcast #205.

Clarence: Jay King from Club Nouveau once gave me the greatest advice. He said, "collect the pennies," and a bell went off for me. I had sort of been doing that, but he really spelled it out for me! "Collecting the pennies" actually meant a lot of things for me.

With royalties, keep an eye out for every penny that's coming through. It could be a $2 check or it could be a fat five figure check, but make sure that it all gets collected.

On a creative level, it means to be flexible when you work with clients. Do something great, but be flexible with the budget and the scope of the project. This approach attracts higher volumes of clients, leads to long term relationships, and potentially future work.

With regard to royalties, it's important to keep an eye out for every penny that's coming through. It could be a $2 ASCAP distribution or a fat five-figure check for a TV license, but whatever it is, make sure that it all gets collected. This helps keep tabs on the real value of a song over time, especially for publishing purposes.

There are many ways to make money in the music business, and the revenue streams in the business are wider and more diverse today compared to the traditional models, so it's just a matter of acknowledging change and making sure the monies are all collected correctly and arrive in your mailbox. The pennies tend to add up, and truly help with sustaining ourselves in the business for the long run!

———

When Your Accounts Work, You Work

#89: Joe Sublett

Saxophonist Joe Sublett is a Grammy and W.C. Handy Award winner, as well as an inductee to the Blues Hall of Fame. His credits including work with superstars like The Rolling Stones, Eric Clapton, Bonnie Raitt, Little Feat, The Band, Stevie Ray Vaughan and Double Trouble, BB King and a host of others. Joe's advice comes from Inner Circle Podcast #207.

Joe: When I first got out to Los Angeles I was talking to another saxophone player on a session who'd been around for a long time. I said, "I'm new to town, so do you have any advice for me?" I thought he was going to give me some jazz player kind of "Here's what you do on this altered chord" kind of thing, but instead he said, "Here's the thing, when your accounts work, you work. When they don't work, there's nothing you can do." An account is the cats that hire you. When they work, so do you.

When you're working and making big dollars you have to act like you're making small dollars.

Another thing is when you're working and making money, you should be putting some money away, because when the time comes when you're not working you're going to be real happy that you didn't spend it all when you were making it.

That's one of the most important things that a professional musician needs to know. When you're working and making big dollars you have to act like you're making small dollars. I thought about that ever since. When it rains, it pours, but when it doesn't, it's really dry. You have to be smart about your bread.

Taking Care Of Business

The music business is just that - a business. If you want to make a living in it you have to know how to navigate it.

Although some of the advice in this chapter at first looks to be specific to the music business only, you'll find that it all applies to just about any kind of business that you might undertake.

Don't Be Afraid To Fail

#90: Jeff Ponchick

Following a job overseeing music partnerships at independent YouTube network Fullscreen, Jeff Ponchick founded Repost Network in 2015. The Los Angeles startup now helps some 3,000 musicians monetize their streams on SoundCloud and elsewhere. His advice comes from Inner Circle Podcast #22.

Jeff: Don't be afraid to fail and don't be afraid to do it yourself. You learn more from those types of experiences.

It's all about finding gaps and filling them since the world's a screwed up place and there are lots of gaps to fill. If you're young and can take the risk, take it.

It's all about finding gaps and filling them since the world's a screwed up place and there are lots of gaps to fill.

——

It's All About Street Smarts

#91: Jamie Pupora

Jamie Purpora has spent a lifetime as an executive in music publishing, first as a senior VP of Administration at Bug Music, then as president of music publishing at Tunecore, and currently as the president of copyright and royalty administration at the digital collection reproduction agency Audiam. His advice comes from Inner Circle Podcast #25.

Jamie: Getting the money is all about street smarts. I've had employees that have gone to college or business school or a music school, and when they get here, I have to teach them how to be street smart.

It's all the sequence of events. What's the other party going to do to not have to pay you? What are they going to use as an excuse to not cut the check? If you don't always send all the information required, be it tax information, or a letter of direction, or a signed document, and crossing all the "t's" and dotting all the "i's," then you're not eliminating all the ways for them to get out of paying you. And it's all street smarts.

> *If you don't always send all the information required, …then you're not eliminating all the ways for them to get out of paying you.*

A professor can tell you about it, somebody can write a book about it, I can throw all these funky terms at you all day and night, but the bottom line is that you have to outsmart the sources that owe you money.

They're not all out to rip you off, but they're doing the best they can for their clients or companies as well.

They have things in place that they can only do things based on the systems that they have, and you have to think what's the best way to make things easier for them so I can get paid. When you're changing a tire on your car, you don't jack the car up without loosening up the lug nuts first. It's the same kind of thing here as well.

———

Create A Solid Business Plan

#92: Pete Lyman

Pete Lyman is a co-owner of Infrasonic Sound, and has mastered projects for Jason Isbell, Chris Stapleton, Weezer, Panic! at the Disco, Fall Out Boy, Rival Sons and Sebadoh to name a select few. His advice comes from Inner Circle Podcast #26.

Pete: I feel like I learned a lot of lessons the hard way. I think if you're going to start a business, then come up with a solid business plan. I was really lucky when my partner Jeff and I started the studio together.

What we did was max out our credit cards and bought a lot of gear, then went down to Home Depot and bought a lot of stuff so we could build the studio ourselves. I don't recommend doing that [laughs]. If I could go back and change that I probably would, but I made it through and learned a lot. We got lucky that we didn't make too many mistakes.

> *Don't overextend yourself. Do good work and the gear will come.*

Before you go out buying things, come up with a business plan and make sure you're not over-extending yourself. Gear is great, but gear is not what's really important. The most important thing is your ears and the room.

Concentrate on that before you go out and buy stuff. Don't overextend yourself. Do good work and the gear will come. Most clients don't care what gear you have anyway. The most important thing is the results and that's what you should focus on.

———

Work With People You Trust

#93: John Jennings

John Jennings is a long-time musician and one of the co-founders of microphone manufacturer Royer Labs, where he currently serves as VP of Sales and Marketing. Many believe the rebirth of ribbon microphones in modern studios has been a result of his personal efforts. His advice comes from Inner Circle Podcast #30.

John: I was talking with a business advisor regarding a company I was involved in that didn't work out. One of the reasons why it didn't was because a partner I was involved with wasn't as honest as I would have hoped. The advisor said to me, "You learned the most important thing. If you have the trust, you have everything. If you don't have the trust, you have nothing."

He had originally advised me against getting involved with this company, but he said, "You know, you didn't lose much, and you learned the most important thing." It was really a great piece of advice.

> *You don't always want to work with people that you agree with because you ideally want someone bringing different ideas to the table…*

You don't have to always agree with your partner, but if you trust him and know his heart's in the right place, that means everything.

You don't always want to work with people that you agree with because you ideally want someone bringing different ideas to the table (often times that means admitting that their ideas might be better) and then you find that place in the middle where the ideas come together.

Work with people you trust. If you have trust issues, either work them out or move on.

———

Take Some Business Courses

#94: Francis Buckley

Engineer Francis Buckley has engineered for the likes of Quincy Jones' various productions, Alanis Morissette's big hits, and even punk pioneers Black Flag. His advice comes from Inner Circle Podcast #33.

Francis: I don't know that this came from any particular source, but it came from many sources, including my mother when I was getting ready to go to school and she said, "Take some courses in business." I said, "I don't need courses in business. I'm in music, so I don't need that."

> *I always ask young artists, "What are you going to do with your record when you're done?", because if you don't have a plan, nothing is going to happen.*

Learn the business part of things. You can't just assume that your record is going to take off. I always ask young artists, "What are you going to do with your record when you're done?", because if you don't have a plan, nothing is going to happen.

If you want an example of why it's important to learn the business, The Beatles didn't do it, and Paul McCartney is still fighting for ownership of his songs all these years later.

You really need to understand this because there's no record company that will do it for you, and even when there was, it was more likely that they were doing it to you rather than for you.

———

Make More Money Than You Spend

#95: Hanson Hsu

Hanson Hsu is a cutting edge studio designer who's taken the art of room design and acoustics to a new level. His Delta H Designs company has done acoustic consulting for Yahoo Music, Mike Shipley, Universal Mastering, Alan Meyerson, McGill University, Pepperdine Music Lab, Dan Wilson, Yahoo Nissan Live Sets, Ryan Hewitt, SAE Los Angeles, Hyperloop Technologies and Aerospace Technology Corporations among others. His advice comes from Inner Circle Podcast #35.

Hanson: If I had to put it in layman's language it would just be "make more money than you spend." I know that sounds ridiculously simple, but you can translate it into do you're accounting well, get paid up front, or vet your clients well, but in short, don't get so lost in your craft that you can't pay the bills.

> *...don't get so lost in your craft that you can't pay the bills.*

I know a lot of famous and really incredibly brilliant savant creators, engineers, producers, artists, electronic designers who have gone bankrupt. You just have to be pragmatic about it and make sure you have more money than you spend.

――

Fail Fast And Move On Quickly

#96: Scott Page

Not only has Scott played with such seminal bands as Pink Floyd, Supertramp and Toto, but he's also quite the entrepreneur as well, having started a number of tech companies, one which even went public! How many rockers do you know that have rung the bell of the New York Stock Exchange? Well, Scott has. His advice comes from Inner Circle Podcast #58.

Scott: My biggest advice today for artists is they need to think like a startup business and use the processes that are well-defined in today's business world.

One of the things that I'm most excited about in that world is the lean startup movement. The reason is that it's a process to build a business that focuses on reducing risk. It allows you to really formulate your idea to make sure you're going down the right path without running out of resources.

I've started 7 different companies so far, and I've had some wonderful successes and some horribly painful failures. The ones that failed had a common thread - I never really tested my idea properly. You get what they call "the founder's dilemma."

In your head you can see that everybody wants what you're creating and how it's the greatest idea and if you build it they will come, but the best thing I could tell you is to don't do that! Stop! Go Back! That's a hits game.

---

*The ones that failed had a common thread
- I never really tested my idea properly.*

Now a lot of people are talking about the principles of lean startup and tweaking it to fit different genres, just like I have. The whole idea there is for you to create your hypothesis, test it, quickly build an MVP (minimal viable product), get it out into the world, measure the results, learn what you can do better, and then change it as needed. You fail fast and move on quickly.

That's actually some great advice. Fail fast. Don't get discouraged but use it as a valuable tool that will help you move forward on your idea.

How does that apply to music? Here's what I tell artists these days. You want to make an album? That's a lot of work. Are you sure that people are going to want that album, especially in a world where it's all about singles?

I'm not saying that you shouldn't make art and create your vision, but spending 6 months on creating a full-blown album today (especially if you don't really have a market for it yet) I don't believe is wise decision unless you're in it for art's sake only. You're better off to keep on writing tunes, and start getting a feel for what's going to work and finding out who's your core audience and what they care about. I'm not saying that you shouldn't be true to your heart because it could be the kiss of death if you're not, but you can do this so much smarter now.

I recommend that you read *The Lean Startup* by Eric Reese and *Running Lean* by Ash Maurya. These books will change your thinking on how to approach your business, and yes, as an artist you are a business. Then go to leanstack.com, set up a free account and create a lean canvas. This is a one page business planning tool used a lot in Silicon Valley (it's my favorite business planing tool, but be sure to watch the videos on how to fill it out first).

The important part of doing a business canvas is not only that it will help you focus on what to do, but most importantly, what not to do. This really gives you a much better chance for success.

———

It Takes Time To Develop

#97: Shan Dan Horan

Over the past decade, Shan Dan Horan has worked for labels Century Media, Republic, Universal and Fearless, and was president of Artery Records. He now heads Outerloop Records. His advice comes from Inner Circle Podcast #69.

Shan Dan: The best advice I've received is that it takes time to develop something. It really helps to have a 5 year plan. If I talk to any band I tell them to formulate a 5 year plan, because nothing happens overnight.

> *Don't get discouraged if you're not a success right away because most things take time.*

The difficult thing is that a lot of young bands are programmed to think that it just happens instantaneously, thanks to some "get rich and famous overnight" Hollywood movies. You just keep working towards a goal, figure out a 5 year plan, and then at the end of that plan you're going to have a successful release.

Don't get discouraged if you're not a success right away because most things take time.

Read Your Contract

#98: Michael Beinhorn

Producer Michael Beinhorn is one of the most interesting people in the music business, having worked with artists like the Red Hot Chili Peppers, Soundgarden, Herbie Hancock, Korn, Ozzy Osbourne and more. He's also author of a great book called *Unlocking Creativity: A Producer's Guide To Making Music And Art*. His advice comes from Inner Circle Podcast #88.

Michael: Read your contract [laughs]. Don't get yourself into anything that you're going to regret later on, and make sure that you know exactly what you're preparing to sign on for.

I know so many people (and I'm a prime exponent of this by the way) who will sit around, mulling over something for long time and weighing out the pros and cons. Meanwhile, there are red flags going up everywhere, which are blithely ignored and at the end of a day or so of deliberating, they go, "What the heck - I can do this!"

Look at each situation carefully, weigh out the pros and the cons, and if something smells funny to you, follow that lead.

I have often dived into a situation, believing I could fight the good fight, but then, a couple of months down the road, I would find myself going, "What the hell did I get myself into?" [laughs heartily]

Look at each situation carefully, weigh out the pros and the cons, and if something smells funny to you, consider that feeling carefully. Don't let the part of you that says, "I'm a man. I'm strong enough. I can do this" have the absolute final word. That part may be right, but if it's wrong...

———

Never Say No To A Gig

#99: Phil Rohr

Engineer/producer/bass player Phil Rohr specializes in recording both audiobooks and long distance (like from L.A. to Australia) film and TV ADR, a couple of jobs that few in the audio business are ever exposed to. His advice comes from Inner Circle Podcast #92.

Phil: Never say no to a gig, no matter how small it may seem. I'm one of the main connections for a lot of Australian TV production companies because about 6 or 7 years ago I got a call from an Australian guy who needed to do 15 minutes of voiceover to send back to Australia. He told me that it was going to happen once a week. He gets the script, he reads it once, and I send it over the Internet back to Australia.

He was broke, but the deal was that he could keep this job (which was from Australia but he had only recently moved to L.A.) as the voiceover guy if he could find a studio in L.A. that could do the work.

He said, "I can pay you 20 bucks." That was way less than I was used to getting, but I thought to myself, "Why not." I had nothing booked on that day and I had to be in the studio anyway.

I set up a mic and he came in and did it, and it turned into a weekly thing. Then one day I get an email from someone in Australia looking for a studio that was referred to me by this guy.

Now the production companies in Australia are only together for one project at a time, so everyone moves on to another one after the show is over, so when the production supervisor was looking for someone to do ADR, she called me. So now I'm working with two different production houses, one in Melbourne and one in Sydney, and now they call me when they need somebody in Los Angeles.

It's your own fault if you jump into something and don't manage to pull it off because you weren't prepared for the job.

As a result, I've done about 15 different television shows for the Australian market and I see them now on Netflix, and it all started because I didn't say, "Nah, it's not worth my time." That was an important lesson, because before that I used to say no to those types of jobs. I don't know how much work it might've turned into, but in this case, it turned into a lot.

Another thing is I guess you'd say "Be Prepared."

When you get that call to do a voice over or audio book or ADR or something, you know what that job is.

ADR is very specific. When I first started I researched different techniques and how various studios did it just because on my very first job I wanted them to walk in and think that I had done it for years.

You don't get a second chance if you mess up doing something like that. So do your homework, which is so easy to do now with YouTube and all the online resources, there's no excuse to be surprised, certainly technically. It's your own fault if you jump into something and don't manage to pull it off because you weren't prepared for the job.

———

Think Of The Client

#100: Larry Crane

Larry Crane is the editor and founder of Tape Op magazine, the owner of Portland's Jackpot! Recording Studio, a freelance engineer, and the archivist for musician Elliott Smith. His advice comes from Inner Circle Podcast #97.

Larry: You have to think about the client all the time.

When you come into my studio, on the back of the producer's desk is a USB port and power strip, because the first thing they have to do is plug in to recharge phones and computers. There are extra charging cables available for different types of iPhones. There's a ¼-inch jack so they can plug computers or phones in to play over our monitors from back there. There's a printer/scanner in the front room to copy lyrics or print sheet music. There's filtered water, tea, and coffee. These are very practical things, but half the time I go to another studio, none of it's in place.

My place may be a lower budget studio than L.A. or NYC, but the artists' needs here are always taken care of.

My place may be a lower budget studio than L.A. or NYC, but the artist's needs are taken care of.

—

Start Crazy And Work Backwards

#101: Rick Barker

Rick Barker helped launch the career of Taylor Swift as her first manager and served as the social media mentor on the hit television show *American Idol.* He offers a great *Social Media For Music* course full of tips and tricks on how to use Facebook, Twitter and YouTube to help you promote your music. His advice comes from Inner Circle Podcast #101.

Rick: Scott Borchetta [Taylor Swift's current manager and label president] taught me early on to start at crazy and work backwards.

One of the things, and it kind of tied in with a philosophy that I had always had, was "weird wins." And the reason that weird wins is because 98% of folks won't get out of their comfort zone, so that means that if I'm willing to get out of my comfort zone, I only have to outwork two percent. I like my odds with that.

> *98% of folks won't get out of their comfort zone, so that means that if I'm willing to get out of my comfort zone, I only have to outwork two percent.*

When I had an idea to do my program a lot of people said it was crazy. They said, "No, you should just go out and find the next artist." Well, then I'm at the mercy of their success in order to provide for my family.

I wanted to find a way that I could be in the business that I love, where I could provide a service, and because I'm able to provide that service, I'm able to then provide for my family. So, I did start at crazy and I work backwards and every day I'm doing weird things, and it's suited me well. It really has.

—

Stay Out Of Debt

#102: Manafest

Chris Greenwood goes by the stage name of Manafest, and has released eight critically acclaimed studio albums that have either won or been nominated for a host of GMA and Juno awards. Chris has also written a book and created a number of online music business courses designed to help up and coming musicians learn the ropes. His advice comes from Inner Circle Podcast #107.

Chris: Stay out of debt and plan.

Run your business debt-free, and plan ahead.

When I got signed, I just thought things were going to happen, and I just kept swiping that credit card, and swiping that card, thinking that things were going to happen - and they didn't. It's great to be dreaming, but sometimes you just have to say, "What is actually going to work here?", and be a little smarter with it.

So those are the two biggest things. Run your business debt-free, and plan ahead.

Pace Yourself When Buying Technology

#103: Michael Perricone

Michael Perricone is not only a movie and television re-recording mixer (meaning post-production mixer), but a musician and screenwriter as well. He's worked on tons of movies and television shows, and has mixed a number of music episodes involving Heart, Cheap Trick, ZZ Top and many others. On top of that, Michael was also a writer for the Star Trek Voyager show, His advice comes from Inner Circle Podcast #108.

Michael: Don't to try to keep up with technology at every moment and pace yourself as far as technology expenditures. It keeps moving fast but if you're getting a good product with what you have, just wait a little bit until cash flow catches up before you buy the next piece of gear.

A lot of times things would come up on ebay and I'd say, "Oh, that's a great deal, that would really ...." Well, there'll be another one later on. It may not be the right time to do that now.

It [technology] keeps moving fast but if you're getting a good product with what you have, just wait a little bit until cash flow catches up before you buy the next piece of gear.

———

Find Your Mission In Life

#104: Joey Sturgis

We've met Joey before in Advice Tip #11.

Joey: There's something that clicked for me the last couple of years that has made everything so much easier, and that's finding my mission in life. Basically if you can find your mission and can summarize it in one sentence so you can tell people what you do in that one sentence, and it's not too specific and it's not too broad, you'll be able to do a lot with that.

One of the things that I ask myself every day regardless of what I'm doing, if I'm watching a video, or adding a post or replying to a comment, I'm thinking to myself, "Does this go with my mission? Is this aligned with what I'm here to do on earth?" If it doesn't, I stop doing it immediately, and I turn to things that are more beneficial to me and to others that benefit from my mission.

...if you can find your mission and can summarize it in one sentence so you can tell people what you do in that one sentence... you'll be able to do a lot with that.

So for me it's to help people to make great music, and I try to make sure that everything that I'm doing is tied to that in some way and helping to push that forward. It's a way to strengthen your core offer or core skill or core product or core value - whatever it is, if you can tie everything you do into it, you're just going to make that thing so much more valuable.

I think that if you can get into the mindset of thinking that way, it will make you successful.

———

Find Out Who You Are

#105: Roger Linn

Roger Linn created the first modern drum machine that used real drum samples, and actually changed the face of music, since so many of hits have incorporated his LM1, LinnDrum or MPC. Roger's also a recording engineer, guitar player, and even an accomplished songwriter, writing hits for both Eric Clapton and Mary Chapin Carpenter. His advice comes from Inner Circle Podcast #111.

Roger: I was never that much of a businessman and I'm still not. I think it's important to find out who you are and make sure your business reflects that. I don't really like running a big company. When I had my first company I had as many as 55 employees and it was just chaos.

At heart I'm still a musician, but instead of making songs or recordings now I'm making instruments. I like to work alone so I actually have no employees, but what I do have is a company I work with that does all the manufacturing for me and some people that help me out with software. It's all very scalable, and coming from being a musician, scalability is important because there are lean times and there are good times. So it's good not to have heavy expenses when things aren't moving along so well.

> *You have to find out who you are and*
> *structure your business around what*
> *you want to do with your time, because*
> *you are going to have to be spending*
> *your time at it.*

You have to find out who you are and structure your business around what you want to do with your time, because you are going to have to be spending your time at it.

Someone said that "If you own your own business you work half-days - 12 hours." Another one that was good was, "When you own your own business you get to choose when you want to work. You can pick any 18 hours you want per day."

But if you love it, it doesn't matter. You're getting paid for your hobby.

———

It's Not The Gear

#106: Ed Cherney

Ed Cherney has become one of the legends of the studio end of the music business, having won 3 Grammys, an Emmy award, 5 TEC awards and been inducted into the TEC Hall of Fame. His client list is a who's who of great artists that include Bonnie Riatt, The Rolling Stones, Eric Clapton, Bob Dylan, Willie Nelson, Elton John, Bob Seeger, Sting, and even Spinal Tap, among many more. His advice comes from Inner Circle Podcast #120.

Ed: Bruce Swedien always said, "Nobody leaves the studio dancing to the console," which has been great advice. People think it's the gear and it's not that at all. Nobody leaves the studio dancing to the gear.

Run it [your career] as a business and run it responsibly no matter what's going on in the background.

Swedien also imparted on me that I should run my career like a business and that meant paying my taxes and having my billing and business stuff in order.

When you make money, save it and don't be a schmuck. And I did that. Invariably all of us go through dry periods where you have weeks or months where the phone doesn't ring, and because of that advice I've been able to weather those periods and not have to get rid of my house or live in my car or have the IRS breathing down my neck.

Run it as a business and run it responsibly no matter what's going on in the background. I've seen too many people who have blown through everything they ever made and are left with nothing at the end of the day.

———

Bend Your Idea To What The Market Wants

#107: Dave Kusek

Dave Kusek has been a pioneer in the digital space in many ways, going way back as one of the creators of the Synare (the first electronic drum) and later the first computer sequencer with Passport. Dave was also the creator of Berklee Online, one of the first online education programs in the world, and now teaches music business with his own courses with New Artist Model. His advice comes from Inner Circle Podcast #125.

Dave: Charles Kaman (of Kaman Music) was a bit of a mentor to me. Charlie was the guy behind Kaman Music. He was an aerospace guy and created the round-back Ovation guitar with a couple of his engineers almost as an experiment.

He once told me that if you're going to be successful, it's going to take twice as long as you think it's going to take, it's going to cost twice as much or more than you think, and it's going to end up being for something other than you started out trying to make.

> *...if you're going to be successful, it's going to take twice as long as you think it's going to take, it's going to cost twice as much or more than you think, and it's going to end up being something other than you started out trying to make.*

I've actually found that to be true most of the time. Certainly it always takes more time and money. But the big nugget in there is that it's going to turn out different than the vision that you originally started out with.

The reality about being in business is reacting to your market and customers and bending your idea to what the market really wants. I've found that to be true over and over again in my career.

Don't Be Afraid Of Risks

#108: Brian Schmidt

Brian Schmidt is a legend in game audio. Both a composer and sound designer, he has worked on over 150 games, and he's been the architect for the X-Box audio system and XACT gaming audio tool. Brian is also the founder of GameSoundCon, a conference exclusively for game audio professionals. His advice comes from Inner Circle Podcast #127.

Brian: Don't be afraid to take some risks, and that goes across all the different disciplines. Not just creative risks, because you don't want your demo to be Hans Zimmer clone #17, but also don't' be afraid to take some career risks. For me that meant that in 1989 I quit my job at a game company that I really loved to become a free-lancer.

> *Take some risks in all the different aspects of your career whether its creative or business, because nothing is going to happen unless you jump off the cliff.*

Take some risks in all the different aspects of your career whether its creative or business, because nothing is going to happen unless you jump off the cliff. There may be something really cool that you land on that will eventually take you up to a higher peak.

Your Passion Is What's Important

#109: Dirk Ulrich

Dirk Ulrich is the founder of 2 great music plugin companies, Brainworx and Plugin Alliance, but his journey into software development involved an extensive stint as a producer and studio owner first. His advice comes from Inner Circle Podcast #132.

Dirk: When I was running my studio and my little label and publishing company I was really trying to plan for success. We had to borrow some money so the bank wanted business plans and all, but even with that, I always survived but I never made a lot of money. The funny thing is that when I started something that I didn't even see as a business in the beginning, which is plugin development, that's when everything began to take off.

...if you have a passion for something and get good at it, this is the best way to get ahead.

So follow your dreams or your passion because this is what's important in the end. It's the opposite of this tendency for everyone to have startups with the idea that they can sell in a couple of years. That's like gambling really. For a few people this might work, but if you have a passion for something and get good at it, this is the best way to get ahead.

You Can't Do Just One Thing

#110: Jordan Young

Engineer/producer Jordan "DJ Swivel" Young has worked worked with mega-artists Jay-Z, Kanye West, The Chainsmokers and Fabolous, and was Beyonce's engineer and mixer for a number of years as well. His advice comes from Inner Circle Podcast #137.

Jordan: In this business you can't really do just one thing. You can, but it's risky, so I try not to put all my eggs in one basket anymore. For example, if your gig is with one artist and your entire income is from there, you have this risk that the artist might want to take a break or go on tour, then you're on your own.

...you need multiple income streams, especially in music.

To take that a step further, you need multiple income streams, especially in music. There are so many opportunities. I've diversified from being just an engineer and producer to starting a tech company (SKIO Music), a magazine (Headliner Magazine), and a publishing company.

They're all still in music, but they give me new creative outlets which are exciting, and they've each helped to create ancillary business opportunities stemming from them as well. Each of these play well off one another and have done wonders in both defining, and building my brand.

———

Don't Spend Your Time On One Project

#111: Joshua F Williams

Joshua F. Williams is a producer/recording engineer from Los Angeles currently based in Dubai. He has worked with artists such as Fergie, Bruce Springsteen, Flo Rida, Stevie Wonder, J.C. Chasez (of N'Sync), Akon, Lumidee, and has worked on many award winning projects that have garnered three Avima medals, two New York Film Festival Gold medals, and the Sound and Stage award. His advice comes from Inner Circle Podcast #146.

Josh: A couple things. Back when I was assisting (producer/engineer) Steven Stewart Short in Los Angeles, he told me, "Don't spend all your time on one project and spend years on it because you'll miss on a lot of other projects that you could have done that might have done better for you." I really do believe in that so I always try to get as much work as I can.

...keep on working to get there - do it well, but do it efficiently

---

I remember that you [Bobby Owsinski] always used to ask when I was assisting you, "Is it soup yet?" whenever there was a technical problem.

What that meant was to keep on working to get there - do it well, but do it efficiently. That's something that I try to do in business.

———

Think Of Yourself As A Business

#112: Michael Carey

Michael Carey started his career as a guitar player, but soon found his way into writing music for commercials. His credits include Toyota, Ford, Sonic, Coke, Papa Johns, NASCAR, Exxon, and Outback Steakhouse among others, as well as on-air promo packages for CBS, NBC and TBS. His advice comes from Inner Circle Podcast #149.

Michael: If you're doing this professionally there are things you can do to market yourself effectively. We really have to think of ourselves as businesses and apply those business principles to what we do. You have to figure out what is your strong suit and what do you have to offer, and how you can then speak to the people who need what it is what you do best. How can you communicate with them and start those conversations and demonstrate what you have to offer.

> *You have to figure out what is your strong suit and what do you have to offer, and how you can then speak to the people who need what it is what you do best.*

All of the discipline that I learned doing commercials proved to be really valuable when I started getting more into songwriting and the production side of things. For a long time I had been apologetic about doing music for commercials and things that I should have been proud of. Coca-Cola and Exxon and Ford and beers and cars and steaks, yet I was sort of grumbling inside saying, "Well, I'm not really making the records that I want to be making."

I ended up learning skills and disciplines that were so applicable when I started focusing more on recording work. Because I continued to stay in touch stylistically and continued to do sessions (as a guitar player), that brought a contemporary sensibility to the commercial work.

Now I just look at work as "work." I don't draw lines between commercials or television or albums or songwriting. It's just, "What's the mission and how can we make the best thing that we can?" Every piece of work is going to be the thing that defines you until the next piece of work that you do.

———

Focus On What You Have

#113: Dane Meyers

Dane Myers created a company called Custom Tracks that allows you to submit your song to a crack team of studio professionals that will then craft it while you watch and listen online in real time. His advice comes from Inner Circle Podcast #154.

Dane: What comes to mind is that there's a prominent servant in the startup community here who had a really successful hair care business that she had started. Her mentality was that there's so much that's possible now because of all the resources that we have.

Even if you're not born with a silver spoon in your mouth, the disparity in resources is small between the average person and someone that's well funded.

> *Even if you're not born with a silver spoon in your mouth, the disparity in resources is small between the average person and someone that's well funded.*

Focus on what you have and take advantage of all the things that are out there instead of letting what you don't have get in the way.

Even companies with huge resources have this come into play because we subscribe to the idea that we still need something else to be successful. In the end it's the value that we put in and not what we consume what other people are making for us.

Find out what pains people are experiencing that you can try to work out a solution to. If you can do that it's a really happy life and a good experience too.

———

Have A Sense Of Consistency

#114: Gavin Lurssen

Gavin Lurssen started as a protege of the great mastering engineer Doug Sax (the very first indie mastering guy) but quickly forged his own way and sound, first at the famed Mastering Lab, then at his own Lurssen Mastering in Hollywood. Along the way he's mastered projects for everyone from Foo Fighters, Queens of the Stone Age, Eric Clapton, Sheryl Crowe, Miranda Lambert and Elvis Costello, among many others, plus he's won 4 Grammy awards for his work. Gavin also now has his own mastering plugin from IK Multimedia. His advice comes from Inner Circle Podcast #156.

Gavin: We have doctrines that we live by. Things like consistency being at the forefront. If you come to us and you only have a little money and aren't a household name, we give the same treatment that we'd give anybody else. When you have that sense of consistency, the world gets to know you in that.

What I've noticed is that those who tend to favor someone who's famous and a big client and treat them differently tend to have a shorter lifespan in the business, so consistency is a crucial aspect.

> *Whatever it is that's coming in to your life, you kind of have to balance it with what's going out of your life as well.*

And it's not just for selfish purposes, there's something greatly satisfying about being consistent. It promotes a sense of self. It's a meditation because it allows you to live in that moment all the time.

Another thing we pay attention to is the the give/take cycle. There are people in life that are takers. "How much can I get?" Then there are people who are just givers, and that's unsustainable as well.

I think you have to pay attention to the cycle of releasing and receiving information, money, equipment or whatever it is that's coming in to your life. You have to balance it with what's going out of your life as well. What that's going to do is to keep you in the community.

Interacting with one's community and knowing why you're doing it and setting your strategy for doing it is very important for being successful in any line of work, whatever your industry is. It's a service and at Lurssen Mastering we all as a crew enjoy being of service.

———

Understand Positioning

#115: Eric "Mixerman" Sarafin

Engineer Eric Sarafin has had great success with artists like The Pharcyde, Tone Loc, Ben Harper, Lifehouse, Bare Naked Ladies, Amy Grant, and Foreigner, among many others. He's a great engineer/ producer, and certainly deserves all the accolades that he's received for that, but you might know him better for his writing under the name of Mixerman. His hilarious *Daily Adventures of Mixerman* book is a must read for anyone in the business, as are his *Zen and the Art of Mixing, Zen and the Art of Producing,* and *Zen and the Art of Recording* books. His advice comes from Inner Circle Podcast #162.

Eric: My advice would be to understand positioning and what it is. Positioning is a business term. In cars, Volvo positions itself as a safe car, and Lexus positions itself as a luxury car, BMW positions itself as a sporty luxury car. They compete against each other but they compete towards a niche.

You as a business operator have to understand what your position is and what your branding is and make your decisions based on where you want to go.

For instance, if you don't like editing drums, then don't edit drums. If you don't like music that's to grid, then don't start working with bands that want to be to grid, because that's what your life is going to be from now on.

> *You as a business operator have to understand what your position is and what your branding is and make your decisions based on where you want to go.*

You have to be very cognizant and careful about the gigs that you take, and that's difficult when your need to take every gig that comes along. You still have to be cognizant of it and make sure that you're not putting yourself in a position that you don't want to be in and might have to try to break out of later.

I positioned myself from the very beginning as a guy who would not be known for working in any particular genre. I wanted to have a super-diverse discography. I would have been way more successful in the short term had I made myself THE guy in a particular genre. I also would be dead broke if I did that because things change, and if you put all your eggs in one basket then you have to completely reinvent yourself, and that's a very difficult prospect. And you have to reinvent yourself all the time as it is in this business. So understand that what you do is what you are. If you do things that you don't want to do, you risk becoming that person.

———

Don't Get Pigeonholed

#116: Shane Theriot

Guitarist Shane Theriot has a lot of experience playing with a wide variety of artists from Beyonce to Dr. John, among many others, but he earned his funk credentials during his 8 years with the legendary Neville Brothers. He's also a Grammy winning producer, and musical director for Hall & Oats and Daryl Hall's *Live From Daryl's House* television show. His advice comes from Inner Circle Podcast #167.

Shane: I don't think there's one piece of advice. There are things that come to mind that are both valid and very useful nuggets, but they often contradict themselves.

I remember a guy in Nashville who was a big session guy that told me once, "Don't get pigeonholed," and that stuck in my mind. And then at the same time I remember hearing "diversify" [laughs].

You don't have to have everything mapped out, but know what it is that you want to do, because it's so easy to wander in this business.

I think they're both valid but it first depends on what you want to do. In this day and age it doesn't hurt to diversify and maybe have some engineering and Pro Tools chops. Some arranging skills are helpful as well as being able to knock out charts. Take some vocal lessons and be able to sing some background vocals. Maybe have a little keyboard chops - things like that.

On the flip side pertaining to not getting pigeonholed, if you want to be a solo artist, then stick to that. I've had friends that just stuck it out and did one thing and now they're known for that one thing. If you want to be a solo artist, that's it - you have to commit to it.

You don't have to have everything mapped out, but know what it is that you want to do, because it's so easy to wander in this business.

———

Learn Some Business Skills

#117: Dusty Wakeman

Dusty Wakeman has had a great career as a bass player, producer, engineer and studio owner, and is now the president of microphone manufacturer Mojave Audio. His advice comes from Inner Circle Podcast #169.

Dusty: I've learned that it's important to learn some basic business skills. When I first owned my studio my business plan was to produce a couple of multi-platinum records and that would be it [laughs]. Even though I had a good run and I'm very satisfied with my career, that never happened.

At one point I woke up and realized that I was a small business owner and I went to the local community college and took two semesters of accounting and a semester of business law. That really changed my life, and I couldn't do the gig I have now without that background.

...you have to have some business chops along with some web and social media skills.

When you learn a little bit of accounting or just basic bookkeeping, you kind of scratch your head and go, "How can anybody function without knowing this stuff?" Because you really need it. You're on your own these days.

Young musicians out there trying to make it, they're a self-contained business. So you have to have some business chops along with some web and social media skills.

———

Get Some Pro Advice

#118: Michael Bishop

Michael Bishop has been recording orchestras all over the world for a long time, first as chief engineer for the famed Telarc label, and now with his own Five/Four Productions. Along the way he's won 10 Grammy's as well as a slew of other awards for his excellence. His advice comes from Inner Circle Podcast #170.

Michael: When we started Five/Four Productions we went to the SCORE program, which is a project of retired business executives, and that was probably one of the best things that we ever did. These retired business executives that were paired up with us were mostly from advertising and marketing. There wasn't anyone from the audio field there, which really didn't matter because we were looking for information on how to build a business.

The advice that they gave was about creating a business plan and making sure that we had a good accountant, and that's been one of the most valuable things to keep our company afloat.

That was really important for us to get started so we didn't just go out there and try a bunch of things that didn't work. We're going into our 10th year now and we went into it without having saved a penny towards building a business. We were all just suddenly out on the street and we had to build something right there on the spot.

The advice that they gave was about creating a business plan and making sure that we had a good accountant, and that's been one of the most valuable things to keep our company afloat.

We networked a lot. I sent out a newsletter both through snail mail and email to a lot of the artists and producers that we worked with. We got the word out as to where we were and what we were doing, and all of our business since then has been through word of mouth.

We all say today that we wished that we had done this 20 years earlier, considering that we started at the end of 2008, right at the end of the biggest recession in modern history. We've never done anything on spec and always get 50% up front and 50% upon delivery of the project.

———

Never Stop Learning

#119: David Scheirman

It's fair to say that AES president David Scheirman is a live sound expert, since he's done everything from mixing bands like America and Electric Light Orchestra to designing sound systems for the New York Philharmonic and the Atlanta Olympics. He's also spent time on the manufacturing side as well in executive positions at JBL and now as director of global concert and rental business at Bose. His advice comes from Inner Circle Podcast #172.

David: Never stop learning. Don't assume that you have gotten to some plateau of knowledge where you're now the expert because this too shall pass. The industry, the tools, the technology are all going to evolve and it's up to you to keep up with them.

I remember lugging my acoustic string bass up and down the stairs when I was in 4th and 5th grade, while playing in junior symphony. Some of my friends were out there playing baseball and making fun of me for being a musician and a music student. I almost quit, but I stuck with it and it led me into a career as a professional bass guitarist.

If I hadn't had those early classical musical experiences as a young man, I never would have accumulated the skills or vocabulary or had the context to be able to satisfy the New York Philharmonic and the Metropolitan Opera in a professionally demanding large scale sound reinforcement environment, many years later.

The industry, the tools, the technology are all going to evolve and it's up to you to keep up with them.

Always retain those interesting experiences that you have because they're like wrenches in your career toolbox for the future. Don't think they don't matter at the time, because they can be the differentiating factor that gets you through a tough decision, or provides an advantage, in your business career. All of those life experiences are things to draw upon in the future.

——

Always Say Yes

#120: Gary Myerburg-Lauter

Gary Myerberg-Lauter has installed and maintained studios for major facilities and superstar artists. Gary's worked at the famed A&M Studios during its heyday, set up a major portable recording rig for Bruce Springsteen, helped run L.A.'s famous Cello Studios then brought it back to life as EastWest, and now manages the technical operations for five of the city's busiest studios. His advice comes from Inner Circle Podcast #173.

Gary: I really believe that there are no studios in existence that I would call "true businesses." I hate the say that but it is true. Every studio that I take care of has some other means of support other than being a studio.

If you always say yes, then you're always going to be successful because the oldest rule for business is that the customer is always right,…

There's only one thing and that is that you always say "yes" to whatever the client that comes into your studio wants. There's never a situation that you say "no."

If you always say yes, then you're always going to be successful because the oldest rule for business is that the customer is always right, no matter what kind of moron they are [laughs].

There should never be anything that you can't deliver to your clients. They recognize that, and in the end they may even pay a little extra to have that. That's the key - just never say no.

———

Surround Yourself With Smart People

#121: Chris Crawford

If you ever recorded a cover song for an album or YouTube you know how time consuming getting a publishing license can be. Loudr makes that process easy for indie artists, and went one step further by taking its technology and making it easier for publishers to get paid from streaming services as well. CEO Chris Crawford has watched Loudr go from a label that specialized in a cappella music to a company leading the technological charge in the new publishing business, and relates the business lessons he's learned in the process. His advice comes from Inner Circle Podcast #174.

Chris: I'd like to think that there's an ah-ha moment every week, or I like to look back and think, "How could I have thought this two years or five years ago?"

For Loudr, one of the most helpful things was that one of our early investors suggested that we put together an advisory board of professionals that we can go to to get a second opinion on tackling something.

A lot of times you don't need to completely reinvent the wheel, you just need to build off what's working. That piece of advice has resulted in so many great things for the company that the value of that suggestion is probably the highest of any suggestion I've ever received over the years of doing this. Basically, surround yourself with smart people.

A lot of times you don't need to completely reinvent the wheel, you just need to build off what's working.

I always hope to be the dumbest person in the room because there's so much to learn from other people.

Also, every time we hire somebody we try to find an all-star that's able to do a specific thing so much better than anything else so that the bar is continually raised. It sometimes makes the earlier employees nervous in a good way, because everyone then steps things up a gear. It keeps us working hard and it keeps us working smarter too.

———

Take Care Of Your Customers

#122: Ben Loftis

You've most likely heard of Harrison Consoles, which were a mainstay in music recording studios in the 1980s and 90s and still dominate in film studios today. You might not be aware that the company also has an excellent DAW with its Mixbus and Mixbus 32C, and Ben Loftis is a product manager for these excellent software products. His advice comes from Inner Circle Podcast #176.

Ben: There's the old adage that "It's better to keep a customer than go find a new one."

There is a problem in today's culture where you use your iPhone for a couple of years and throw it away because there's one that's way better that's just been released.

Pro Tools is another great example. They're pretty aggressive in making sure that you upgrade, otherwise it just stops working.

There's the old adage that "It's better to keep a customer than go find a new one."

Harrison actually has a very long history of taking care of customers in a completely different way. You can go to Universal Studios today and you will be sitting in front of knobs and faders that were originally installed in 1994. It's been upgraded, yet they never had to make that giant capitol investment again. We didn't make them take the whole thing out and put a new one in every 5 years.

———

Business Is A Triangle

#123: Tommy Darker

Tommy Darker is a musician, lecturer at the University of Westminster, speaker at global music conferences, and the founder of Musicpreneur Hub, a global community of music entrepreneurs where you can ask anything about music and your question will be connected with handpicked, top industry experts to answer. His advice comes from Inner Circle Podcast #186.

Tommy: I've discovered that business is a triangle - value, audience and revenue. Business cannot exist without these three elements.

Make sure you know what you're bringing to the table, to which organization or group of people you're offering it to, then how you can have a monetary exchange so you can get revenue.

> *...no matter what you do there is the common sense of what this is, and then there's the vision behind it, which is who you are, what you've studied, and where you want to go.*

The second piece of advice comes from my mentor, who created the first luxury olive oil in the world (Lambda olive oil).

Olive oil is a commodity, yet he turned it into a luxury product. He told me that *"This olive oil is not made out of olives. It's made out of books."* This means that, no matter what you create, there is 1) the common sense of what this usually is, and 2) the unique vision of a person that makes it special (i.e. who you are, what you've studied, and where you want to go).

With this mindset you can turn a commodity product, like olive oil, into a luxury item, with people happily paying a tremendous amount of money to get a small amount of it.

Applying this mindset, you have 'music as usual" (the streams and mp3s out there), and then you have premium music products with a vision behind them.

———

Save Money For Marketing

#124: Brian Calhoun

Bryan Calhoun has been a business and marketing consultant to artists like Kanye West, Lil Wayne, The Cult, Questlove, Nicki Minaj, and Drake. He's a noted music industry speaker, and has given workshops at conferences that include SXSW, MIDEM, CMJ, and over 20 more. Bryan is also the creator of an excellent program for artists and bands everywhere called the *Music Business Toolbox*. His advice comes from Inner Circle Podcast #191.

Brian: The biggest mistake I see is artists allocating all their money to record and then not saving any for marketing.

Understanding how money flows through the industry is super important. Gaining a real understanding about the industry is important too, but be careful where you get your information from because some people have ulterior motives.

> *Understanding how money flows through the industry is super important.*

You want to be armed with that information so that you can make the right decisions for yourself and your situation.

———

Don't Believe Your Own Press

#125: John Mathiason

John started his management career guiding the career of the multi-platinum band Sponge, and later went on to handling the endorsement deals for Soundgarden and Alice in Chains before starting Candy Shop Management with Antony Bland. His advice comes from Inner Circle Podcast #196.

John: I used to do consulting for a merchandising company and the owner of the company said, "This is all you need to know about business." And it was watch your inventory and don't believe your own press.

I think you can apply that across the board whether that inventory is your overhead or the number of people in your band. And then, don't have ego in the game. Those are great pieces of advice.

...you can apply that across the board whether that inventory is your overhead or the number of people in your band.

——

Set Some Money Aside

#126: Billy Decker

Nashville-based Billy Decker has mixed nine #1 hits so far for artists like Kenny Chesney, Darius Rucker, Jason Aldean, Jaime Lynne Spears, and Sam Hunt. His advice comes from Inner Circle Podcast #197.

Billy: If your self-employed, 9 times out of 10 you will be paying quarterly taxes, so I would suggest setting aside some money in a little fund every time it comes in, knowing that you'll need to send it to the IRS. You don't want to ever get behind, because then you just dig yourself into a hole that can be tough to get out of.

...know your write-offs and definitely save money for taxes.

Also, get yourself a good accountant because there may be a bunch of write-offs that you might not be aware of. I lease my studio, so i get to write it off. Know your write-offs and definitely save money for taxes. And never own a studio! it's a terrible investment.

Keep Moving Forward

#127: Roy LaManna

Roy LaManna is the founder and CEO of Vydia, a music video technology platform that allows artists to distribute to networks like MTV, Fuse, BET, and Nickelodeon, and publish their videos on platforms like Vevo, YouTube, and Facebook. His advice comes from Inner Circle Podcast #198.

Roy: Just keep moving forward. That's the biggest thing. Looking backwards you always feel good about what you've done, while looking forward you always feel confident but there's always 10 different things that are on your mind that you think are going to be challenges. When they pop up, you feel like giving up, but the people that make it are the ones that learn to overcome those challenges.

> *"If you can't run, then walk. If you can't walk, then crawl, but just keep moving forward."*

You've got to keep moving forward when everyone else stops. I think it was Martin Luther King who said, "If you can't run, then walk. If you can't walk, then crawl, but just keep moving forward."

People Care About Themselves, Not You

#128: Joyce Kettering

Joyce Kettering is a composer who became so successful in licensing her music that she did the thing that so many dream about - she quit a very good day job as a financial auditor. What makes this all the better is the fact that Joyce lives in Paris, yet most of her placements have come from the United States. Joyce's Music Licensing course outlines everything you need to know to not only get started with licensing your music, but to be successful at it as well. Her advice comes from Inner Circle Podcast #206.

Joyce: A mentor once told me that people don't care about you, they care about themselves. That stuck with me and it's really important. Only when you starting thinking about what your customer needs can you up your game and create something of value. It's applicable to music as much as business.

Only when you starting thinking about your customer that you have to up your game do you up your value.

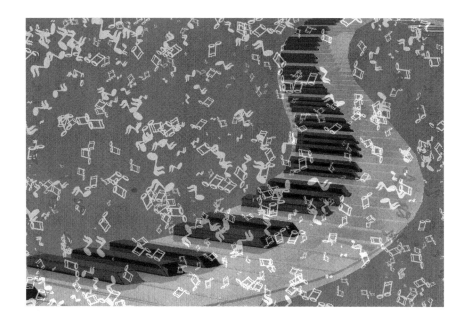

8

Music Gems Of Wisdom

If you work as an artist, songwriter, producer or engineer you'll love this chapter. These are some fantastic words of wisdom involving the creative process that just might get you over a hump or help bypass a roadblock.

Be Consistent

#129: Ed Seay

Ed Seay has become one of the most respected and influential engineers in Nashville, with hit-making clients such as Blake Shelton, Lee Brice, Martina McBride, Ricky Skaggs and a host of others, Ed has led the charge in changing the recording approach in Nashville. His advice comes from Inner Circle Podcast #24.

Ed: When I started out, I sucked, and then I got better. I started to experiment with everything at my disposal, and then I started to suck again because it just sounded really weird. Then I broke through the clouds and got better again and learned from that experience. Then I got really good. A snare or a vocal can only be so good, so the next step from that is to be consistent.

The worst thing is when you're great some days and other days not so good...

I want to hit a triple or a home run every time at bat. I never want to strike out or only get on first. The worst thing is when you're great some days and other days not so good, so the advice is to try to be consistent as well as good.

———

A Guest In Their Creation

#130: Dave Pensado

Over the last two decades Dave Pensado has taken mixing to a new level of artistry, having mixed big hits for superstars like Christina Aguilera, Justin Timberlake, Kelly Clarkson, Pink, Black Eyed Peas, Beyonce, Shakira, and Michael Jackson, among many others. Well known in the business way before his popular *Pensado's Place* web series, Dave is not only on the cutting edge of technology, but has thought long and hard about the more cerebral aspects of mixing as well. His advice comes from Inner Circle Podcast #32.

Dave: For me, no matter how many hits you have or how much success you have, it's still a service industry for us. It's not anything else other than client services. I'm no different than a barber. You come to me and ask me for a haircut, I provide the best service I can and give you the best haircut that I can. I send you out the door and you look like a million bucks and you're happy. I go to a trade show every once in a while and learn all the new haircuts and then try to hip up your look a little bit. It's a service industry.

Always remember you're a guest in their creation, so you want to finish their creation and you don't want to hijack it unless they ask you to (and we get asked that from time to time).

Your pay is always going to lag behind your skill set.

The other advice I would give people is if you watched a YouTube video about how to drive a car around a NASCAR track at 220 MPH, you wouldn't get into your car and try to do that right after you watched the 30 minute video. You might make it a quarter of the way around, but the first turn, you're dead. When we provide information about how to do things, we can shorten the time it will take for you to go 200 MPH, but we can't eliminate it.

You have to have realistic expectations about how you're going to grow and get skills. Be honest with yourself about your skills. If you're not making any money, then that's what you're worth. Your pay is always going to lag behind your skill set. You can't "social media" yourself to the top. All those modern day shortcuts, the only thing that works is doing it, doing it, doing it. Starting out on a go-cart, then working your way up.

——

It's More About Feel

#131: Dennis Moody

We've heard from Dennis previously in Advice Tip #77.

Dennis: I remember very early on doing a session with Charles Wright (from the Watts 103rd Street Rhythm Band). Sonny Burke, an awesome piano player, was producing it and he had just started to take off as a producer. The band came in for a playback and Sonny said, "I just need you to fix this note." They got into a huge debate about fixing stuff with feeling. Charles said, "That's the way I played it. That's the way I felt it. I want to keep it. It doesn't bother me."

I thought, "Wow, he's working with such a great producer. I wonder why he's questioning him? He should just go do it again." Then I thought, "That's really an interesting thing he's doing there."

After that I started noticing that it's more about feel, and you can let some things go. They're not mistakes, it's interpretation. There could be bad notes or bad timing, but if it feels right, it's okay.

> *They're not mistakes, it's interpretation.*
> *There could be bad notes or bad timing,*
> *but if it feels right, it's okay.*

I just did a record with Steve Gadd and it's a total feel record. If you put it up on a click you'd go, "He's not playing in time." But it's perfect the way it is. You couldn't make it any better.

So what I've learned from doing this all these years is that the feel and the vibe of the performance supersedes anything technically.

———

It's Okay To Fire Your Clients

#132: Ariel Hyatt

Ariel Hyatt started her career as a traditional music publicist but dove into online social media soon after it started. As a result, she's become the go-to expert for online PR for artists, bands, musicians, and record labels, as well as authors and entrepreneurs with her Cyber PR agency and several social media guidebooks. Her advice comes from Inner Circle Podcast #55.

Ariel: This is one that took me a long time to really get, and that is it's okay to fire your clients. What I mean is anyone that you serve, so if you're a touring musician you're serving club owners. You're serving anyone that's in some way profiting off of a relationship with you. I could be a manager. You're serving your band members.

In this crazy journey in wanting to succeed, especially when it's around art, it's personal and deeper than a lot of business relationships that normal people in the other world have.

I think that I suffered a lot trying to deliver when I couldn't, or when my client gave me something that wasn't working, or sort of flogging myself and making myself wrong instead of going, "Okay, what if I just walked away from this and we found someone else to do this." Or, "What if there could be something different here." I think that I didn't learn that until I suffered way too much.

...there's power in understanding your boundaries, and when you feel that you're compromising your boundaries and are emotionally drained and you tried your best, it is okay to walk away from things.

People think that it's alway's the publicist's fault, especially when I was a traditional publicist. You can have an album that could be falling flat and the label or management would call and scream. You never know exactly what the fault is. Maybe something else really great came out that week and took all the radio or PR slots, or a tragedy happened in the world and that got all the news coverage. There's a million reasons why things don't always go well.

The best piece of advice is that there's power in understanding your boundaries, and when you feel that you're compromising your boundaries and are emotionally drained and you tried your best, it is okay to walk away from things and to do it with integrity.

If that takes giving back a little bit of the money or admitting you didn't do it as well as you could have, or apologizing or cleaning up your side of the street, that's a really important lesson that I think a lot of us never learn. Many of us don't learn it until we've been kicked around a lot or until we've suffered.

I actually learned that from Michael Port, who wrote a very interesting book that I love called *Book Yourself Solid*, which is about how to find the right people to work with and serve in the world.

———

How Can I Help You?

#133: Garth Richardson

Garth Richardson grew up in the studio thanks to his dad Jack Richardson, who produced Alice Cooper, The Guess Who, Badfinger, Peter Gabriel and Poco among others. After being around music all his life, it's no surprise that Garth has gone on to engineer records for luminaries like Taylor Swift, Red Hot Chili Peppers, Nickelback and Motley Crue, and produce acts like Rage Against The Machine and Mudvayne. He's also one of the founders of the excellent Nimbus Recording School. His advice comes from Inner Circle Podcast #62.

Garth: One is to get a really good lawyer [laughs].

The other thing is that as soon as you sense that there's something wrong with your session, your singer, your drummer, your guitar player, etc, deal with it as soon as it happens.

What happens if you don't is that it's almost like a dike. When that first crack happens, if you don't fix it it's going to become a big crack and then the whole dike is going to fall. Whenever something happens, I deal with it right on the spot right then and there.

> *... as soon as you sense that there's something wrong with your session... deal with it as soon as it happens.*

I do it nicely saying, "I hear that you are having a hard time with this. How can I help you?" All of a sudden, it becomes less of a big deal, and they're going to say, "Wow, that was easy" and then everything moves on, so the biggest thing is communication.

―

Bust Yourself Before Others Bust You

#134: Pete Doell

Pete is currently a senior mastering engineer at Aftermaster in Los Angeles after a long stint at Universal Music Mastering Studios, but he's unusual in that he has a long history as a tracking, scoring and mixing engineer before he went into mastering. In that capacity Pete has worked with a wide variety of major stars including REM, Marilyn Manson, Celine Dion, Los Lobos, Brian McKnight and Dwight Yokum. His advice comes from Inner Circle Podcast #64.

Pete: Always bust yourself before others bust you. If you have reservations or you're not confident that you have the right tool for the job, it's best to share those things honestly and upfront while there's still an opportunity for an alternate solution and nobody's going to hang you for it.

If you try to sweep stuff under the rug or try to be Mister Nice Guy and try to deal with a situation that you knew right away was a recipe for disaster, it rarely works.

> *If you have reservations or you're not confident that you have the right tool for the job, it's best to share those things honestly and upfront when there's still an opportunity...*

That took me a long time to learn. Look, you're not being a jerk. You're being a responsible guy to raise your hand and say, "I'm not your guy," or "This is a problem."

I'm not a confrontational person by nature, but there are times where you have to step up and address the situation.

———

It Will Always Be Alright

#135: Ted Hutt

Ted Hutt started his career as a guitar player for the celtic band Flogging Molly, and eventually became their producer. He's since gone on to produce dozens of acts including Dropkick Murphys and Old Crow Medicine Show (for which he won a Grammy), among many others. His advice comes from Inner Circle Podcast #80.

Ted: Don't stress [laughs], it will always be alright. You have to try to stay away from that place where things start to get weird and make sure not to let anyone panic or stress. The creativity gets closed down real quick when you start getting stressed

---

If something doesn't work, it's better to change directions rather than bang your head against the wall until everybody's done.

You can make that case that everything that goes on in the studio is in a tiny way a microcosm of what goes on in the world. You have to figure solutions to things. If something doesn't work, it's better to change directions rather than bang your head against the wall until everybody's done. You don't need anything that's a negative, so if something's not working, that's a positive cue to change course.

———

Lose The Charts

#136: Paul ILL

You've met Paul previously in Advice Tips #45 and #84.

Paul: This one comes from my original bass mentor in New York City in the 1970s. I took Will Lee's place in the Joe Beck Band and Will and Joe were my heros and mentors back then. Will handed me the charts and said, "Lose the charts before the first gig." I looked at him and asked, "Lose the charts?" taking him literally. He said, "No man. Just don't bring them to the last rehearsal. Leave them home. You'll have a better first gig if you don't bring the charts to the last rehearsal."

You want to play from the heart instead of the page.

In that spirit as a studio musician, if your technique is to chart the music, try to get off the chart as quickly as you can (if you can) while you're recording, regardless of what your chart is. Whatever you're using to cue yourself to remember what you're supposed to play, lose it so you can maintain that fine line between spontaneity and command of the music.

People have varying gifts for their ability to do that. What I try to do is to play without the chart as soon as I know that I'm in the ballgame and understand the song and I know my part. Get off the written page as quickly as possible, and in fact, don't do the first take with the chart if you can.

Never compromise your musicality or the vibe of the session to test yourself in that realm though. You want to play from the heart instead of the page. Get your heart in the music as soon as you can.

Don't Take It Too Seriously

#137: Jamie Oldaker

Jamie Oldaker was a long-time member of both Eric Clapton's and Bob Seger's touring bands, and has also recorded with musicians such as The Bellamy Brothers, Asleep at the Wheel, Peter Frampton, Stephen Stills, Leon Russell, Ace Frehley, Freddie King, and The Bee Gees, among many others. His advice comes from Inner Circle Podcast #98.

Jamie: I've kept my career underneath the radar on purpose because I saw what this [the music business] was early on, and saw how it ruined a lot of people. That's why I chose not to be an out-front artist. I'd rather back people, because I can always play with somebody else. If an artist's career goes down the toilet, they're finished.

But when it comes to advice about business, there's something I've lived by my whole life. When I was 18 or 19 years old, I went to breakfast with a fella here in town that I just met - [legendary artist] JJ Cale. I went to breakfast with him after I played a little bar here (I'd snuck in because I was too young to get in but played anyway), and he knew I was on my way to try and get in this business.

We had some breakfast, and he ordered some pancakes. At that time, he used to wear his hat on backwards, and it had a little feather in it. Down by his chair he had a paper sack with some whiskey in it. And he ordered some pancakes and I was sitting there next to him, and he picked up a syrup jar, those jars with the clip thing on them, you know?

"Don't start believing that crap you're reading in the papers. Don't believe you're Elvis, okay?"

And he pours some of that whiskey in that syrup jar, and then he poured that whiskey and that syrup on his pancakes. He took a bite and he turned around and looked at me and goes, "Don't take this shit too seriously." [laughter] That's the best piece of advice I can give anybody, because if you do, it'll ruin you.

I've told people that many of times. You take care of your business, yes, but don't start believing the shit you read, because it'll be the end of you. Now I've told people that before. I had a band called The Tractors, I told them, "Don't start believing that crap you're reading in the papers. Don't believe you're Elvis, okay?"

———

Know Who To Produce

#138: Ken Caillat

We've met Ken previously in Advice Tip #85.

Ken: For being a good producer, I remember Richard Dashut [co-producer of Fleetwood Mac] said it's as much about knowing who to produce as it is about how you produce.

For being a good producer, ...it's as much about knowing who to produce as it is about how you produce.

———

Good Mental Health

#139: Ed Cherney

We'v met Ed previously in Advice Tip #116.

Ed: I think you need good mental health. Everything in this business is designed to rob you of any slice of self-esteem that you may have. We all get fired, we all get replaced. You may have done the best work of your life and know it and you find you're sending the materials to someone else to remix it or redo it, for whatever reason.

You have to find a way to pick yourself up and do it again and have the same amount of enthusiasm and joy going in and it's difficult.

It happens the same way with artists. I've seen some of the most talented people not be able to get over. I don't know why that is, but this whole thing is designed to rob you of any self-esteem you might have, as I mentioned. At the same time, to do this well you need plenty of confidence.

You especially have to be able to pick yourself up after being fired or failing or not getting hired or being replaced.

You have to find a way to pick yourself up and do it again and have the same amount of enthusiasm and joy going in and it's difficult. So having good mental health is a big part of it.

———

You Can't Rush Quality

#140: Russ Hughes

Russ Hughes has had a successful career in multiple aspects of the music business, but started a small blog dedicated to helping Pro Tools users that has grown into a group of sites (Pro-Tools-Expert.com, Logic-pro-expert.com, Ableton-Live-Expert.com and Studio-One-Expert.com) that may be the most influential in the digital audio world today. His advice comes from Inner Circle Podcast #124.

Russ: You can't rush quality. You can't fake quality. You can't fake a great vocal, for instance. Even though we have the tools now that we didn't have 20 years ago, you still can't fake a great drum performance. It takes skill and talent in both the artist, the musicians, the writers, the engineer and the producer.

> *...if I had to boil it down to just one phrase, it would be "Don't settle."*

In the instant music making society that we have today, we're presenting a story to the new generation of engineers that anything is possible and we can really "fix it in the mix." I don't believe that. I think that real quality shows, and even more than that, stands the test of time.

So if you want to make a career in making music either on one side of the glass or the other, spend time crafting your skills because you're never wasting your time if you do that.

You're wasting your time if you try to take shortcuts, because it will be like a fast food versus a beautiful meal that you'll never forget again. I've sometimes tried to take shortcuts, and I regret it now.

The things that really matter are the ones that I took my time on and didn't settle. So if I had to boil it down to just one phrase, it would be "Don't settle."

———

Let The Song Go

#141: Greig Watts

Music publisher Greig Watts is a co-founder of UK - based DWB Music, which represents songwriters and producers who have had numerous hits around the world including Number 1's and top 10 hits in Europe, the United States and Asia. His advice comes from Inner Circle Podcast #129.

Greg: One of our writers, Ian Curnow, who's written songs that have sold millions of copies, taught me a lesson a few years ago when I was getting too concerned that the artist that was going to cover a song wasn't big enough. He said, "Once you've written a song, let it go."

Your job as a writer is to write the next song. Wherever that song goes, you can't control it, and it could be that a small act that wants your song becomes the next big thing. By you saying, "No, I don't want to do this because they're too small," you've just blocked that.

> *The songwriter's job is to write the next song, because songs have a life outside the studio.*

Our first success in Japan was like that. An act used it and sold 60,000 copies, which wasn't that great, but then it went on another B side that sold 80,000, and then it went on two other albums, which lead to about 250,000 sales. Once you add them all together, we had a very big success. We've had it just the opposite as well where a big artist didn't sell all that much, so just go with it, because you can't control it.

The songwriter's job is to write the next song, because songs have a life outside the studio.

——

The Value Of Listening

#142: Matt Hines

Matt Hines is an audio post production professional, mastering engineer and a product manager for the plugin company iZotope. His advice comes from Inner Circle Podcast #144.

Matt: The value of listening - truly listening - cannot be overstated.

You hear stories of the 'studio rookie' making the tea/coffee, unable to touch a knob, fader, or make any kind of edits until they've earned a holistic and meaningful aesthetic appreciation for the art.

It's extreme, but I was very fortunate to have been put through that.

If you've listened closely, hopefully you'll know what is going to happen before you make that change.

Sitting in recording sessions all day, every day, with every spare evening, weekend and holiday that I had (I was in high school), I so desperately wanted to touch the equipment, but instead spent hours listening to the conversations, and more importantly to the music being made and observing the reactions people had to the music as it grew from infancy to release.

More than ever these days, there's a sense of immediacy, a need for instant gratification. Looking back, the time spent listening to both people and audio was invaluable.

If you've listened closely, you'll have the emotional intelligence to understand, before making any kind of mix and mastering adjustment, why you're making that change and what's going to happen when you make that change.

———

Agents And Managers Work For You

#143: Shawn Mikle

Shawn Milke's band Alesana had been touring almost non-stop since 2004 when he decided to tap the brakes and get off the road for a bit. This resulted in the creation of Revival Recordings, which lives by the inspirational mantra "Good Music By Good People." Now with distribution through Artery/Sony Red, the label continues to grow and prosper despite the indie business climate. His advice comes from Inner Circle Podcast #155.

Shawn: I think it was through a manager I had for very many years who I considered to be my mentor, Eric Rushing. He is the founder of all things Artery. He taught me (and I'll never forget this and still preach it to this day) that as an artist you can't forget that your manager and your agents work for you. A long time ago that might have been clear but there's a guise going on in the industry where it seems like the other way around.

This is a business and people are trying to make money and there are tons of different ways to make money.

The biggest thing I learned from him came one time when he got mad at me and told me I was wrong. That was really when I realized that, "Oh, artists really don't know everything and we're not always right."

Having that understanding was really when I started to dig in on that side of things, taking notes and learning everything I could about the business. I realized that the music industry is just that - It's an industry and it's just like any other business. I studied business when I was in school and I guess this correlation never occurred to me until the first time he gave me a hard time.

This is a business and people are trying to make money and there are tons of different ways to make money. That was actually my "light bulb" moment, when I realized that I could make this a long-term career.

———

Never Say Your Can't Do Something

#144: Sylvia Massy

Sylvia Massy has an incredible resume that covers Queens Of The Stone Age, Black Crowes, Smashing Pumpkins, Johnny Cash, Prince, Tool, Lenny Kravitz, and many more. Her advice comes from Inner Circle Podcast #161.

Sylvia: The best advice is to never say "no" in the studio. If a client asks you to do something and you say "No, you don't want to do that" for whatever reason, that's a terrible thing to do. Even if in my mind I'm saying, "God, no," I'll always be encouraging and say, "Let's try it."

Give them a chance to hear the results, and if it is truly a bad idea, then it will be obvious and they will have learned something. Or if it is a good result, then I will have learned something. I never want to force my production onto an artist, it is not my music. A mistake I've made in the past was telling an artist that they had a bad idea. I regret that and don't do it any more.

If a client asks you about doing something and you say "No, you don't want to do that" for whatever reason, that's a terrible thing to do.

——

Have Their Interests At Heart

#145: Bob Power

Bob Power is a Grammy Award–winning and multi-platinum producer, engineer, composer, arranger, performer, and educator. He was a big part of the second generation of hip hop, working with A Tribe Called Quest, De La Soul, Erykah Badu, D'Angelo and Macy Gray, among many others. Bob has two music degrees, and is also currently a professor at the highly regarded Clive Davis Institute of Recorded Music at New York University's Tisch School of the Arts. His advice comes from Inner Circle Podcast #190.

Bob: I learned that you will successful if your clients know that you will go to the wall for them and you will work twice as hard as they will. Whether you're getting paid a nickel or two million dollars, you have to make sure that everyone understands that you have their very best interests at heart and not your own. There are times when you'll be taken advantage of, but there are many more places where people will appreciate that and want to have you around.

> *...you will successful if your clients know that you will go to the wall for them and you will work twice as hard as they will.*

Being Definitive Is Being Compassionate

#146: Joel Hamilton

4 time Grammy-nominated producer/engineer/ musician Joel Hamilton credits include the Black Keys, Iggy Pop, Elvis Costello, and Pretty Lights, among many others. Joel's also a part owner of Studio G Brooklyn and a frequent speaker at conferences all over the world. His advice comes from Inner Circle Podcast #194.

Joel: Something I learned first and foremost is that the phrase, "Dude, I don't know," has eaten more budgets that anything I can think of. Second guessing every decision in the studio has cost record labels, engineers, producers, bands more money than the cost of any big console you've ever seen. Think about the number of times someone's said, "Dude, I don't know," and you've had to backtrack and have everyone doubt themselves.

People drive long distances and pay great sums of money to be in the presence of confidence.

The thing that I recognized is that we can do something and we can do something else, but we can't do nothing. Kind of like oil paint where it doesn't set until you leave it for quite some time, we're not done until we're done. Just track the idea. The song is 3½ minutes and you want to talk about it for 40 for a part that would've just taken 3½ to do. For me its do the thing, be definitive, and commit to sounds. All my favorite records had commitment in them.

People drive long distances and pay great sums of money to be in the presence of confidence. I think that reads in a record like in the production style and the way that people deliver the message on a microphone - you can sense that. Would you ever pick a take where you thought, "Well, it might rock now"?

Being definitive actually is compassionate. It's not ruling with an iron fist in the studio; it's having compassion for more things than just the feelings of the guy who suggested it. We know that the meter's running and we're draining resources with every minute that I don't say yes or no as the producer. You wind up spending more time on what matters to the song if you make those decisions quickly. You might realize that your decision was wrong, and if you get your ego out of the way, you track over it. Admit that it's not the way to go or do something else but don't just do nothing.

———

Invest In Yourself

#147: Antony Bland

Antony Bland of Candy Shop Management came from the label and publishing world where he ran the international department at Chrysalis Music Publishing. He also served as the the director of A&R at American Recordings for eleven years before heading into management. His advice comes from Inner Circle Podcast #196.

Antony: One of the things that I'm doing more and more of is investing in yourself. It's easy to give up your entire life to an artist. It's easy to fall into the trap of "If only I can make them happy or successful," and you start to lose sight of yourself. That does you and everyone around you and the artist a disservice.

As long as you're invested in your own happiness and well being, and that means taking a step away from this business sometimes, that makes for a better person. I've certainly seen that when I'm stressed or too focused on something, I'm not making the right decisions with clarity.

Sometimes you have to put it away, turn the wifi off and stop thinking about it for a second.

> *If you're obsessed on it [the music business] 24/7 you can't have a very happy life.*

This can be a really brutal business and it can burn you out. If you're obsessed on it 24/7 you can't have a very happy life.

The reason why we're all in this business is because we enjoy it. It's creative, it keeps us young, it connects us with people who are inspiring. Sometimes you have to forget about the minutiae of what an artist is doing or the bad decisions they're making or how much they drive you crazy and remember that it's their art.

—

Patience Is Necessary

#148: Steve Marcone

Dr. Stephen Marcone is Director of the Music Management Programs at the William Paterson University of New Jersey and the author of the excellent book *Managing Your Band*. His advice comes from Inner Circle Podcast #201.

Steve: To me it was this idea of patience. You are a business person and you want something to happen immediately, but it's not necessarily going to happen quickly with creative people, so you really need patience.

Walter Yentikoff (former president of CBS Records) wrote in his book that when the record labels were forced to answer to corporations quarterly, there was no longer any patience and that's what ruined artist development. It all goes back to understanding what real patience in the business means, and how the benefit of patience can really pay off.

You are a business person and you want something to happen immediately, but it's not necessarily going to happen quickly with creative people, so you really need patience.

—

The Product Is People

#149: Dave Philp

David Philp is a professor of Music and Entertainment Industries at the William Paterson University of New Jersey, which has one of the best music business programs in the country. He's also the co-author (along with Steve Marcone) of the 6th edition of *Managing Your Band*. His advice comes from Inner Circle Podcast #201.

Dave: In the music industry the product is people. It's not like you're making boxes or something that isn't alive. It's a creative, thinking emotional creature and you can't force it to create something that's going to generate something that will get a billion streams on Spotify or views on YouTube. You can't force it to be up to do a 150 date tour over the next 18 months.

> *You're dealing with a group of people that all have their own personalities, some of which are awesome to deal with and some that can be moody and awful people.*

You have to deal with the creative juices that may or may not flow with this person and work around it and understand when they're mad and when they're not mad and still somehow generate the revenue that you're supposed to get from this person all the while understanding that this is a human being.

You're dealing with a group of people that all have their own personalities, some of which are awesome to deal with and some that can be moody and awful people. You have to understand everybody but it's all about people.

———

Set Aside Your Ego

#150: Warren Huart

We've met Warren before in Advice Tip #19.

Warren: This can be summed up in a quote from Quincy Jones about Stevie Wonder. He said, "Stevie always leaves enough space in the room for God." What that means is that Stevie Wonder has no ego.

Your opinion as a producer is actually not the important thing. I learned that from working with producers that are the other way around that only have one way of doing things.

As a producer you have to have a massive skill set, but your biggest skill has to be that you have to be able to communicate and get performances from people. I worked as an engineer with a lot of producers who didn't actually know when it was good.

As a producer you have to have a massive skill set, but your biggest skill has to be that you have to be able to communicate and get performances from people.

And Please

I'd Really Appreciate It If You'd Write A Review Of This Book On Amazon

The number of reviews a book accumulates has a direct bearing on how it sells.

Just leaving a review, no matter how short, helps make it possible for me to continue to do what I do.

Thank you kindly!

Addendum: The 10 Rules Of Networking

1. Go places where you can meet players or people who can help.

2. Keep it casual and don't come off as a stalker.

3. Be memorable.

4. Ask a lot of questions.

5. Keep it about them, not you.

6. Have a business card ready, but only give it out when asked.

7. Ask for their card.

8. Know what to ask for if the opportunity arises.

9. Follow up, but don't pitch.

10. Only pitch if they respond.

About Bobby Owsinski

Bobby Owsinski has taught thousands of music entrepreneurs the principles of branding and social media in his coaching courses, and is one of the best selling authors in the music industry with 23 books that are now staples in recording and music business programs in colleges around the world.

He's also a contributor to Forbes, his popular blogs have passed 5 million visits, and he's appeared on CNN and ABC News as a music branding expert. Many of his books have also been turned into video courses that can be found online at lynda.com, and he continues to provide presentations, workshops and master classes at conferences and universities worldwide.

Bobby's blogs are some of the most influential and widely read in the music business. Visit his production blog at bobbyowsinskiblog.com, his Music 3.0 music industry blog at music3point0.com, his podcast at bobbyoinnercircle.com and his website at bobbyowsinski.com. He can be found on Forbes at forbes.com/sites/bobbyowsinski.

Other Music-Related Books By Bobby Owsinski

The Mixing Engineer's Handbook *4th Edition*

The Recording Engineer's Handbook *4th Edition*

The Mastering Engineer's Handbook *4th Edition*

Social Media Promotion For Musicians *2nd Edition - The Manual For Marketing Yourself, Your Band or your Music Online*

Abbey Road To Ziggy Stardust [with Ken Scott]

Music 4.1: A Survival Guide For Making Music In The Internet Age (*5th edition*)

The Drum Recording Handbook *2nd Edition* [with Dennis Moody]

How To Make Your Band Sound Great

The Studio Musician's Handbook [with Paul ILL]

The Music Producer's Handbook *2nd Edition*

The Musician's Video Handbook

Mixing And Mastering With T-Racks: The Official Guide

The Touring Musician's Handbook

The Ultimate Guitar Tone Handbook [with Rich Tozzoli]

The Studio Builder's Handbook [with Dennis Moody]

The Audio Mixing Bootcamp

Audio Recording Basic Training

Social Media Promotion For Small Business and Entrepreneurs *The Manual for Marketing Yourself or your Business Online*

Deconstructed Hits: Classic Rock Vol. 1

Deconstructed Hits: Modern Pop & Hip-Hop

Deconstructed Hits: Modern Rock & Country

The PreSonus StudioLive Mixer Official Manual

You can get more info and read excerpts from each book by visiting the excerpts section of bobbyowsinski.com.

Bobby Owsinski Lynda.com Video Courses

Audio Recording Techniques

The Audio Mixing Bootcamp

Audio Mastering Techniques

Social Media Basics for Musicians and Bands

Bookmarking Sites for Musicians and Bands

Blogging Strategies for Musicians and Bands

YouTube for Musicians and Bands

Twitter for Musicians and Bands

Mailing List Management for Musicians and Bands

Website Management for Musicians and Bands

Facebook for Musicians and Bands

Mastering For iTunes

Music Studio Setup and Acoustics

Selling Music Merchandise

Selling Your Music: CDs, Streams and Downloads

Bobby Owsinski Online Coaching Courses

The following can be found at BobbyOwsinskiCourses.com:

101 Mixing Tricks

The Music Mixing Primer

Vocal Mixing Techniques

Music Producer Formula

Brand Your Music Crash Course

Music Prosperity Breakthrough

Ultimate Mixing Bootcamp

Editing Tricks Of The Pros

Vintage Gear Mixing Tricks

✦

Bobby Owsinski's Social Media Connections

Music Production Blog: bobbyowsinskiblog.com

Music Industry Blog: music3point0.com

Inner Circle Podcast: bobbyoinnercircle.com

Forbes blog: forbes.com/sites/bobbyowsinski/

Facebook: facebook.com/bobby.owsinski

YouTube: youtube.com/user/polymedia

Linkedin: linkedin.com/in/bobbyo

Twitter: @bobbyowsinski

Website: bobbyowsinski.com

Made in the USA
San Bernardino, CA
01 March 2020